Become A
Confi-Dance

To Richard & Victoria,
Thank you for sharing
time and conversation with us
"old folks". I hope you will
bring dancing into your lives — you
will never forget it!
All the best,
Paul

stardancer@gmail.com

Become A Man of Confi-Dance

Dance your way to self-esteem, happiness, romance and adventure

Raoul Weinstein

To order additional copies of this book, contact:
Xlibris Corporation
1-888-795-4274
www.Xlibris.com
Orders@Xlibris.com
116060

Contents

ACKNOWLEDGEMENTS 11
INTRODUCTION   (The Benefits of Making
                 This Book Your Friend) 13

Section One

SELF-ESTEEM The Road to Confi-Dance

1.   Where I'm Coming From May Be Where You've Been 19
2.   Quick Overview: How I Got Here...24
3.   I Was Born At The Age Of Fifteen 26
4.   BMOC or MOC? (Big Man on Campus
     or Man of Confi-Dance) 30
5.   Wives May Come And Go But Dancing Never Leaves You........32
6.   And All I Have To Do Is Dance With The Ladies? 35
7.   The Young And The Innocent 48

Section Two

HAPPINESS Live Better, Live Longer

8.   Okay, Maybe It's Dancing With One Special Lady.....................57
9.   A Specific Example Of One Specific Dance 61
10. Here I Am, Show Me How It's Done 64
11. Join The Group—There's Safety (And Savings) In Numbers.......70
12. Outsiders And Insiders—A Vast Difference...............................74
13. You Don't Have To Be A Boy Scout To "Be Prepared!".................79

Section Three

ROMANCE: It Will Always Take Two to Tango

14.   We Will Have These Moments To Remember............................87
15.   The Viewpoint If You're From Venus 93
16.   The Viewpoint If You're From Mars..97
17.   Can The Planets Possibly Be Aligned? 100
18.   Be Friends On And Off The Dance Floor 104

Section Four

ADVENTURE: The World Can Be Yours

19.   The Art Of Being A Dance Host...109
20.   I Can Dance—So What Else Do I Need?..................................116
21.   Let's Take A Break And Visit The Confessional Booth.............125
22.   Whoa, You Mean There's Even More To Being A Dance Host? .130
23.   Do I Have To Be Out On A Rocking Ship? 139
24.   Many Nice Guys Do Finish First 147

Section Five

The Dancer's World

25.   The Dancers' Rules Of Etiquette...159
26.   The Aura Of The Man Of Confi-Dance 163
27.   A Good Chapter In A Dancer's Life 166
28.   Combining Dance With Career And Travel Can Be Fun...........170
29.   Competitions: The Path To Fortune, Fame, And Focus............177
30.   To Walk The Walk, You've Got To Look The Look 182
31.   Life Is A Dance, So Dance For Life...186

APPENDIX A: A Waltz, By Any Other Name, Is Still A Pleasure.......189
APPENDIX B: Dancing: Here's To Your Health 195
Index...199

Learn how YOU can bring immense joy and happiness into your life (and the lives of those around you) by becoming confident enough to dance that one special dance in your life or to dance confidently for the rest of your life.

DEDICATION

To Nancy McMillon, who helps fill my life with self-esteem, happiness, romance, and adventure both on and off the dance floor.

ACKNOWLEDGEMENTS

M ORE IMPORTANT THAN anything else influencing my interest in writing a book about dancing are the wonderful ladies I have danced with over the years, far too numerous and obviously impossible to list here. But in particular, my former wives Linda and Susan, my ex-fiancee Barb, and my fiancée Nancy each played a major role. They all love to dance, and in turn helped me love to dance, each in their own style and manner. Much credit also goes to Mary Dague, my dance instructor in Lakeland, FL, who taught me most of what I know about ballroom dancing and supplied the time and space for me to grow those skills. Opening the door to a dancer of my emerging skills and creating for me an unbelievable opportunity to find self-esteem, happiness, romance, and adventure on the high seas as a gentleman dance host were primarily Elly Engberg, Wendy Olsen, Lennie Corbett, and Terri Lynn Goodrich.

Special thanks are due to Jan Scalisi who edited my book originally and made important suggestions as to layout, tone, style, and cohesiveness. I am also in debt to my sister Karen Witte and to my fiancée Nancy McMillon for reading and critiquing the manuscript and for subtly steering me in the right direction at important junctures. And finally, the old adage that says "don't judge a book by its cover" may often be true but when my cover was designed by my own very talented son, Craig Weinstein, that fear was immediately removed.

INTRODUCTION

(The Benefits of Making This Book Your Friend)

"If to dance is to dream, then you make dreams come true."
—Anonymous

I F YOU FOUND out your son was telling his friends, "My dad is a cruise ship gigolo," what would you do? What I did was just smile. Why?

Since 2003, I have had unbelievable and fantastic opportunities to travel the world as a gentleman dance host on many of the finest cruise ships sailing the seven seas. I have competed many years at the United States Amateur Ballroom Dancing Association (now USA Dance) level, I have taught dance classes and workshops, I have met and made lasting friends, I have been attracted by and attracted to various ladies on cruises, and I am now engaged to a lady I met on two separate cruises three years apart, all because I became what I call a Man of Confi-Dance. *Dancing can enhance or breathe new life into a long-term relationship or help ignite a new and exciting one.*

The guys on *Dancing with the Stars* aren't the only ones *scoring* 10s with 10s on the dance floor—men should stop watching and make this a hands-on (your dance partner) experience. More men need to find the enrichment that dancing, not watching, brings to their lives and the lives of those around them. Becoming a Man of Confi-Dance *can* and *will* change your life—it did for me—whether for one shining moment, or for the rest of your life, and perhaps with some 10s along the way.

There are books available that tell you how to dance, from basic steps to advanced, intricate patterns, some with CDs of dance music, and some with DVDs for visuals. However, this book addresses a level before learning to dance: it's the level of *wanting* to learn to dance. It helps men of all ages see a picture of why they should be dancing, what dancing can bring to their lives, and *where* becoming a confident dancer can lead.

The *smile* on the face of a *daughter* or *wife* when you dance with her for the first time at a *wedding* or an *anniversary* will stay in your hearts and memories for the *rest of your lives.* And if you continue to dance for years and years, the joy that will brighten your life will enhance your self-esteem, and your relationships (current and future) in a powerful way a nondancing man cannot know or imagine.

Reading Become a Man of Confi-Dance *is just as vital for ladies whose husbands or significant others won't dance.* It can change the attitude of the man in her life regarding dancing. Every guy who watches *Dancing with the Stars* dreams of holding one of those gorgeous professional dancers in his arms. Yet a man does not have to be a superstar dancer to be a Man of Confi-Dance in the eyes of his lady—he just has to take her onto the dance floor. If he will do this for her, he will find he is also doing it for himself, and there just may be new and exciting doors opening for him and for his relationship.

The joys and benefits of knowing how to dance confidently can be an enormous enhancement to a man's life. Boys not yet in their teens, high school guys, young men in their twenties or thirties or forties, men in their midlife years, and even seniors in their retirement years—this book is addressed to you (and to the women in your lives).

Many men probably know some of the marvelous benefits of dancing already. You may know this, not because you can dance, but because you can't dance. You have watched men who can dance and observed what some have achieved. This is being an outsider, someone who hasn't the confidence to ask someone to dance and enjoy the feeling, the exuberance, the sweet vibrations, and the sense of accomplishment that you and your partner will experience while dancing.

Are you a man whose life is in a rut, not going the way you want it to? Are you stagnant, looking for something new? Is your relationship with your significant other flat, with the same old, same old all of the time? Do you admire the way other men seem to have it all going for them? Do you frequent bars and lounges but shy away from talking to or dancing with the women you see there? Does your self-esteem need a pick-me-up at this stage of your life? Being able to dance confidently made a big change in my life and in the lives of many men I've met and talked to over the years. It just might be the right time for you.

Ladies too can get much from reading this book. How is that possible? Even though a lady does not want to become a Man of Confi-Dance, she just might want her significant other to become one. If you are a lady who'd like a man in your life to become a Man of Confi-Dance, who do you think is going to benefit from this besides him? You, of course! You might have a son, a brother, a father who is recently divorced or widowed, or a favorite nephew or uncle who needs to build his confidence on the dance floor, maybe for one special event or for the rest of his life. Reading this book might very well be the best chance you ever have of finding the right reasons and the right road to follow to finally get the nondancing man (or boy) in your life to learn, and love, dancing—and, most likely, with you!

Become a Man of Confi-Dance has a vast potential audience; it should be read by any man of any age in any country ready to change his life, or by any woman who wants the man in her life to dance with her. The world today, now more than ever, promotes, encourages, and idolizes dancing. According to noted Austrian-American novelist Vicki Baum, "There are shortcuts to happiness, and dancing is one of them." This timely book is that shortcut; it is the key to a man confidently unlocking the door and stepping out (with his baby) into this new and exciting world.

I have divided my book into five sections: "Self-Esteem," "Happiness," "Romance," "Adventure," and "The Dancer's World." These are the areas in which dancing confidently can make the greatest impact in your life. Is there anyone who can't improve his self-esteem, who wouldn't like more happiness, who wouldn't jump at the chance for more romance, or wouldn't love to add a bit more adventure to his present life? I have attempted to group each of my ideas and topics into the one section that each fits with best, but some may straddle the line between more than one. You may want to read it in the order in which it is presented, but you may also enjoy jumping in and out of the sections in the order that may be dictated by your particular interests. Read on. Then dance on!

Section One

SELF-ESTEEM
The Road to Confi-Dance

S ELF-WORTH, SENSE OF worth, confidence, and self-respect might all come to mind when we think of the meaning of self-esteem. Some of us have a lot of it, and some of us are sorely lacking it. And while there may be many ways a man can build his self-esteem, the ability to dance confidently with women has always been at the forefront in most societies as a yardstick with which we measure ourselves and are measured by others. When I first learned to dance in high school, my self-esteem jumped several notches and has increased noticeably over the years as my ability to dance got better and better. It was a long but interesting and enjoyable road to reach the level of confidence I now possess, and I'm delighted to share it with you over the next few chapters.

CHAPTER 1

Where I'm Coming From
May Be Where You've Been

"To sing well and to dance is to be well educated."

—Plato

I WAS INVITED TO go with Dancers at Sea, a company we'll learn more about later, that brings gentlemen dance hosts to dance with the ladies in the group on cruises. This was a cruise around the British Isles aboard the Cunard Line's new and elegant cruise ship, the *Queen Victoria*. It was the captain's cocktail party in the Queen's Lounge, and the evening was called the Black-and-White Ball. I entered the lounge dressed in my tuxedo with matching black-and-white striped bow tie and cummerbund, plus black-and-white, wing-tipped dance shoes. The seven-piece orchestra was starting up, and the spacious dance floor was noticeably empty. The gathering crowd congregated around the edges conversing and sipping champagne, all dressed to the nines. One might think the dance floor was a fearful, off-limits place to be.

The first song was a perfect tempo foxtrot that I enjoy dancing, so I looked around and spotted several ladies in long evening gowns chatting and sipping from elegant goblets that appeared to be without escorts. I walked up to one beautiful lady with a stunning hairdo, lavish jewelry, and a plunging neckline; smiled at her; and asked, "Would you like to dance this wonderful foxtrot with me?"

She smiled back, nodded her head, handed her flute of champagne to one of her friends, and walked onto the dance floor and into my arms. I led her around the perimeter of the floor, not concerned in the least that we were the only dancers on the floor. Here we were, out on the high seas on a magnificent vessel, superb music filling the air around us, and I had a fabulous lady in my arms.

It is a moment of sheer pleasure for a Man of Confi-Dance, a time when ordinary moments are transformed to the extraordinary, and one to share with and be remembered by his partner. My partner seems to feel her connection to Cinderella, and my joy is being a part of this process. The ecstasy is heightened by the knowledge that my dance partner and I are utterly aware that after one or two turns on the dance floor, almost every other lady in the ballroom is watching us and probably thinking, *I wish I were out on the floor dancing in the arms of that fine dancing gentleman,* or perhaps, *I wish this lug standing next to me would take me out on the dance floor so we could look like that, but he doesn't dance.* And in this manner were the seeds planted in my mind to write this book.

Man of Confi-Dance (MOC) with fellow dance host Mario Avila

I can't think of many moments in my life where my self-esteem has been higher and my sense of accomplishment greater. Dancing has brought this to my life, but it wasn't always this way or this easy. The road to self-esteem may be a short road for some and a long road for others. Let's begin a journey along the road that I took that brought me to the level described above. Perhaps you can recognize the road you have been on and be ready to map out the best route for you to take from where you are now to where you might want to be: a Man of Confi-Dance, I hope.

It has been said that a person's number one fear is public speaking. I remember Mr. Addison's sixth-grade class at Walter Reed Middle School in Newport News, Virginia, where my greatest fear was being asked to stand in front of the class late on any given Friday afternoon and sing a song. That fear, and later on the fear of public speaking, were my number one and number two fears. But if we just ask the guys, I would imagine that many would list dancing with a girl or a woman at the top of the fear list. Yes, I've been there too. In Ms. Baker's seventh-grade class at the same school, I recall being chased around the room by a female classmate because I was too scared to partner up with her in some dance class on a rainy day in the auditorium.

With the popularity of television shows such as *Dancing with the Stars*, *So You Think You Can Dance*, and their spin-offs in other countries, dancing has moved back front and center into our society and our lives again. We are watching and we are thinking, *Man, I'd like to dance like that.* But let's face it: We're not all going to be able to dance like the pros do, nor like many of the stars who spend hours each day with professional trainers and choreographers to perform just one dance on live TV that will last maybe two minutes. But they sure look good.

Still I want you to consider this: It's neither too late, nor too early, to add the enjoyable dimension of dancing to your life, to your persona, to a relationship (current and/or future). This new dimension can provide so much pleasure and adventure, and open doors of opportunity that will last for the rest of your life. It did for me.

If you are not in a relationship with a lady, this may very well help you develop one. If you are in a relationship, would dancing spice it up? Is dancing, or the lack of it, something that she has brought up to you, perhaps more than once? Is dancing with you something she wants in her life (i.e., meaning your life) as a couple?

Having recently reached a major milestone in my life, I can look back and ponder the many things that might have turned out differently if I had made different choices. You don't have to live as long as I have to recall a few in your life either, I'm sure. But let me dwell on one particular decision that I made early on that could have been different: dancing. It was certainly the right decision, though it sure took a while for me to find out what dancing could bring into my life. What I've learned can be helpful for boys or men of any age, for males from eight to ninety-eight, and at any level of dance competency. There are many guys that are just as good or even better ballroom dancers than I am now, or ever will be, and if you are one of them, please continue reading. You will learn how I was lucky enough to fall into several niches that have enriched my life because of my ability to dance, and I want you to have the chance to experience the same enrichment in your life. I'm inviting you here and now to become a Man of Confi-Dance, and I'm going to tell you why and how.

I've been a ballroom dancer for about twenty years and have taken many lessons during this time from various teachers. That doesn't make me the greatest dancer by any means, but I do well enough to have finally become what I like to call A Man of Confi-Dance. Perhaps this book will be your moment, a challenge that one day causes you to reflect and say, *That was my moment of awareness, awakening in me an innate desire to become a Man of Confi-Dance.*

> Definition: Man of Confi-Dance (noun): A man of any age, who can ask almost any lady (or a specific lady), to do almost any dance (or a specific dance for a specific moment), at almost any place that you could dance (or a specific venue for a specific event), in a successful and confident manner for the enjoyment of both himself and his dance partner.

Any man can become confident on the dance floor. Becoming a Man of Confi-Dance at any age can open many doors (and windows), bring fulfillment that will surprise you, take you to many exciting places, allow you to meet many wonderful people, and perhaps even help you find a partner for part, or all, of your life. I can attest to all of the above. And in the words off the pen of the famous British writer Jane Austen: "To be fond of dancing was a certain step towards falling in love."

I enjoy having the confidence, the ability, and the opportunity to create enriching moments in my life such as these and to provide memorable moments for the ladies I dance with. I don't mind having the floor all to myself and having others watching what my dance partner and I can accomplish. But I should also like my dancing to be the spark for an observer to take charge of his life and get enthused about dancing. I want this book to give you hope and a realization and awareness of the pleasures and the incredible rewards available to you when you become a Man of Confi-Dance too.

MOC dressed out for formal night

CHAPTER 2

Quick Overview: How I Got Here

**"Those who dance are considered insane by
those who can't hear the music."**
—George Carlin

DANCING DIDN'T REALLY enter my life until I was in high school, but when it did, it came in with a bang and changed my life. I have not let go to this day and, for all these years between, I have thoroughly enjoyed dancing of varying kinds and styles. I have depended on dancing for many venues of social entertainment and personal pleasure and have used dancing to meet girls (at first) and ladies (as I got older). Over the years, dancing seemed to differentiate between those girls or ladies who would remain in my life for some period of time and those who wouldn't. Perhaps it sounds rather harsh and chauvinistic. But it just seemed to work out that way—when I was attracted to a girl or lady and found we danced well together, that added a dimension that endeared her to me that was missing with nondancers. It didn't hurt either if she was cute or nicely put together! But her dancing ability still seemed to be the tiebreaker, the deal maker, the deciding vote if everything else was the same. I couldn't help comparing her to the others I was dating at any given time.

My first wife, Linda, and my second wife, Susan, were excellent dancers. Whatever style was popular at the time or in the places we lived, we wanted to be able to participate. In high school, it was mostly fast dancing, usually some type of swing, jitterbug, bop, or combinations of one or more. We also did plenty of close dancing, slow styles that ended with a dip if you really wanted to show off and impress your partner.

Over the years and with each of my two marriage partners, I danced whenever the opportunity presented itself: weddings, bar mitzvahs, social events, parties, dances, night clubs, cruises, etc. In the early `90s, Susan and I were introduced to ballroom dance lessons (which I will tell you about in more detail later), and that heralded a new era of my life where dancing was a major facet of my social life. Later, when I became single again, I dated a lady whom I knew from ballroom dancing. We became competitive dance partners which eventually led to our engagement for a period of time. After our breakup, I retired and found a new and most extraordinary opportunity which I have been able to continue and pursue to the present day: being a gentleman dance host on cruise ships (like Jack Lemmon and Walter Mathau in *Out to Sea;* let's hope I have better dance technique but alas, fewer Hollywood escapades to share).

I find that many men finally make it to the dance floor because of a woman. It usually takes a good woman, a strong woman, and a woman who knows how to convince her husband/boyfriend/significant other that he'd like to learn to dance, and say to him, "So let's begin with some lessons." There's a good chance you've had that happen to you. What was your response? Did you capitalize on this golden opportunity or shrug her off? Remember, doors will open, good things will happen, when you please the lady in your life who wants you to dance with her. My current partner has often said to me, "A man simply cannot outgive the love of a woman. When he gives her the things (not just trinkets) that make her happy, she will give back to him more and more." I smile just thinking about that. Arthur Murray dance studios had a billboard on the interstate near Orlando, Florida, showing a couple dancing, with the caption, "Do it for her. The rewards are endless." Powerful message!

At each measurable stage of my progress in the world of dancing, I have continued to work and practice my skills at dancing until I became a Man of Confi-Dance. As a man reading this, you may find similar times in your life that mirror mine and had to make a choice of commitment. Either you want to be a Man of Confi-Dance, or don't care one way or the other. Perhaps other pressing issues take priority for a time. Either you reap the rewards of being a Man of Confi-Dance, or it doesn't make any difference. You may have decided that you are not someone who could become a Man of Confi-Dance. I say whatever your age is right now, as long as you are in reasonably good physical shape, there is still time to be that Man of Confi-Dance if there is a desire to be. Let me tell you in more detail how it happened to me.

CHAPTER 3

I Was Born At The Age Of Fifteen

**"You don't stop dancing from growing old;
you grow old from stopping to dance."**

—Anonymous

THAT'S RIGHT, I was born at the age of fifteen, or so I've always claimed. It happened during the summer after my fifteenth birthday when I crashed a sweet sixteen party with my friend, Lewie Ellis. We both were working that summer at the amusement park in Buckroe Beach, Virginia. He went to Hampton High School with the birthday girl which was invitation enough for us to show up at the rooftop ballroom of the Chamberlin Hotel in Old Point Comfort, Virginia. That night, for the first time, I heard real doo wop rhythm and blues music and saw the current dance trends of my fellow high school students. From that night on, life has never been the same.

I heard R&B artists such as LaVerne Baker, Shirley and Lee, Nappy Brown, and Gene and Eunice. Then I raced out and bought their 45s the next Monday at the local record shop. Today, I have a vinyl collection of more than one hundred thousand records, and those original 45s are in an honored place in my collection. I've always enjoyed the old doo wop groups and the great '50s and '60s music, but I also like just about every other kind of music too. And I especially enjoy danceable music.

MOC spinning his old 45s at sock hop

So what was I doing for the first fifteen years of my life that this casual event suddenly changed my life so much? Well, for one thing, I wasn't dancing. Most guys can probably look back at some dance lesson held in the basement or gymnasium of the school we attended where, at the delicate age of between ten and thirteen, we were expected to pair up with one of the girls (yuck) lined up on the other side of the room and dance. Talk about finding the universal way to turn guys off of dancing for the rest of their lives! Who is socially ready for that? What guy has confi-dance to take on that task or the nerve to handle it?

But what if at this age you could have had the confi-dance to take that scenario in stride? What if you had been introduced to dancing in a comfortable setting by someone you trusted, like one or both of your parents or an aunt or uncle or big sister or brother? Can you look back now and say, "Yeah, I could have survived that ritual and developed a little style?" And if so, perhaps you would have stood out somewhat in the eyes of the girls. Not another nebbish like the other guys but someone with pizzazz.

Think that's too early in life to worry about standing out with style? Let's face it, a guy who becomes cool sometime later on is deep down someone who always wanted to be cool at any age. He had the nerve, the talent, or the opportunity to single himself out from his peers in one area or another. For many, that avenue is sports.

My family moved from Philadelphia (how about those Phillies the past few years, huh?) to Newport News, Virginia, and I skipped most of the third grade and thus was a year younger than most of my classmates now in the fourth grade. I was smaller and less mature than most and usually followed whatever the older guys said and did. When I was around twelve or thirteen, the Jewish Community Center I went to with other kids my age brought in a ballroom dance instructor who taught some of our parents (mine included) to teach us kids some basic ballroom dance. Bowing to peer pressure from the other guys, I certainly wasn't going to look like this was something I wanted to do. Not to mention that this guy was a bit dainty and actually wore a sport coat and tie! So when my classmates pooh-poohed the idea of learning to dance at these lessons, I was certainly right there with them—anything to be loyal and one of the guys.

A lot of those guys today are still pooh-poohing dancing because they never learned along the way for one reason or another. I know because I see them at high school and fraternity reunions still sitting on the sidelines when the great music of our times is played and I'm up dancing. In retrospect, I blew an opportunity right then and there that took me another forty years to make up. However, luckily for me, I did make it up. Like the famous line from Marlon Brando in the movie *On the Waterfront*, "I coulda' been somebody" if I had learned even a little something about ballroom dancing then, but hey, who knew? I know now.

When I entered high school, and before I had my own car, I would take the city bus to Newport News High School for dances from time to time. I watched all the cool guys dance with the good looking girls while I sat there all night wishing I could be like them. Of course, they were not doing ballroom dancing, rather the latest dance fads such as the bop, the dip, and a hybrid form of swing not too unlike the shag from the nearby Carolinas. Can you remember doing the same thing because you didn't know how to do the current dances and were afraid to try? A Man of Confi-Dance at that age would be as cool as any guy there. Like my teammates on my high school track team during my last two years, dancers also come in all shapes and sizes. Likewise, a Man of Confi-Dance can dance competently with girls or ladies of all shapes and sizes, and for me now, of all ages too. Remember this: The best-looking woman in the whole room at a dance just wants to dance and will dance with almost any guy who can dance competently and confidently with her. Just ask her. You never know what will progress from just one dance!

Finally, during that summer of my fifteenth year—you know, the year when I was born—I learned enough of the current dance fads to hold my own on the dance floor. For the rest of the summer until school started in the fall, my crowd had parties at somebody or other's house most nights. And when I got my own car—you could drive at fifteen in Virginia in those days, and I earned enough money working that summer to purchase a '47 Dodge Coupe with vacuum shift!—I used to frequent the record stores hoping to be the first among my peers to bring the newest R&B hits to the parties. We danced, we smooched, we laughed, and we cried to all those wonderful songs that summer, and when school started and the first dance was held after a football game, I was there. I was dancing, and though I didn't know it yet, I was on the road to becoming, at least for the moment, a Man of Confi-Dance.

Early in my senior year in high school, we seniors gathered in the auditorium one morning to vote for our class members who would comprise our hall of fame: best looking, best student, best athlete, best dancer, etc. I came in second in the voting for best dancer to a fellow trackman, Jerry Saunders. I never forgot this for two main reasons: how much I had progressed in a little over a year with dancing, and that I came in second, not first!

At the forty-fifth and fiftieth reunions of our class, Jerry was there, and so was I. Jerry could see how much I had progressed in my dancing over the years. It was a nice feeling, although it still didn't make up for the vote of our class back in high school. From conversations with Jerry, I concluded that we had both danced with a lot of wonderful ladies in our lives and had both derived our share of happiness, enjoyment, and high moments over the years. Our abilities on the dance floor had provided each of us the opportunities over the years to be Men of Confi-Dance.

This book is not to convince you that if you learn to dance, you will have more women than you can handle. It is not to tell you that dance venues are good places to connect with women. It is not to point out that men who can dance are at a premium and command a lady's attention. It is not to make you believe that dancing is the foreplay that leads to the bedroom. What this book intends to show you is how much you can and will add to your life through dancing by improving your self-esteem and increasing the probability of bringing a higher level of happiness, romance, and/or adventure into your life than you've ever known before. And very often, the road to romance begins on, or runs right over, the dance floor on its journey there.

CHAPTER 4

BMOC or MOC?
(Big Man on Campus or Man of Confi-Dance)

"Life may not be the party we hoped for,
but while we're here we should dance."
—Anonymous

I T DIDN'T TAKE long for a trend to begin, a trend that followed me for the rest of my life. As I alluded to earlier, every major girl or lady in my life was someone with whom I enjoyed dancing. In high school, there were Joyce, Shyrli, and Lynda. And in college, it was Jackie, another Joyce, and then another Joyce, and another Linda. And it's still that way, but more on that later.

There is something about the sheer exhilaration and instant—even if just for the moment—bonding that happens when you and your partner polish off a dance in style, whatever dance it may be. Fast dances seemed to be the standard of measurement during those high school years, not that the slow songs weren't fun too, especially when you had more than a casual interest in your dance partner. But a girl who could move, a girl with fast feet who could do the jitterbug-like fast dancing that we preferred during those years, was a keeper. Little did I recognize at the time that the reverse would become evident, maybe even more so, because quite frankly, even back then the number of willing and able female dancers far outnumbered the willing and in particular able male dancers. Good dancing men would fall into the keeper category for women. To be a high school Man of Confi-Dance certainly established its own level of coolness. And I knew it.

Putting those 45s on my old turntable in my bedroom, pulling open the two closet doors that had mirrors on the inside at just the right angle, and practicing current and new moves to the music was not only a good workout, but paid dividends many times over at the next dance. You didn't have to be clairvoyant to know that other girls were watching you dance and wanted to dance with you when you were on top of your game. And guys, that hasn't changed for all the years of my life, nor for all of the venues everywhere that dancing goes on. But let's go back to my evolution.

College turned out to be more of the same, but with more hormones and testosterone mixed into the equation. I kept up with my music, continued adding to my record collection, and stayed on top of the dance fads. The underlying dance that always separated the men from the Men of Confi-Dance continued to be the fast dancing. Once you established yourself in that area, you became a Man of Confi-Dance wherever you were: a fraternity party, a party at someone's house, a beach party, a hayride, whatever, dancing put you into the category of cool. A Man of Confi-Dance was in a way a Big Man On Campus. And each girlfriend I had in college was a good dance partner. Was it why I liked them? Was it a prerequisite? I think it's just a hormone-charged ritual of the day that provides a measure of why you enjoy being with each other and keeps your relationship exciting. There'll be more on that later too.

During my senior year in college, I met Linda, the young lady who would become my first wife four years later. And yes, dancing was a prime ingredient. She had danced from the age of three and knew a lot of ballroom dancing (that I had not yet learned) and had fast feet. And yes, she was darn cute too. Our first date was a blind date, set up by my fraternity brother Bobby Hyman's girlfriend, Margie, and was our fraternity's fall hayride. I had been drinking beer a good part of the afternoon (having dropped off the university's track team after my junior year and now trying to drink enough beer to make up for the three years I didn't partake in it), And after we got out to the barn in the countryside where we danced, I was still downing the beer. Well, I can't hold my alcohol, never could, and before long, I was out in the pasture for the rest of the evening throwing up, leading to another one of my fraternity brothers having to take her home with my car as I was still out of it.

But when I apologized to her the next day and asked her to our fraternity's Untouchables party coming up in two weeks, she surprised me by accepting. Why? It turned out that she was impressed with our dancing before I took leave for the pasture. And similar to the phrase Humphrey Bogart used in *Casablanca*, that was the beginning of a wonderful relationship.

CHAPTER 5

Wives May Come And Go But Dancing Never Leaves You

"Dancing is a wonderful training for girls; it's the first way you learn to guess what a man is going to do before he does it."
—Christopher Morley

DURING OUR MARRIED years, Linda and I always loved to dance whenever and wherever the opportunity arose. We didn't work on our dancing, we didn't take lessons, and we never practiced. We just danced those dances (swing, cha cha, a little rumba, twist, etc.) that we knew all along. We were good at it, but we never embarked on any program to improve or get better. I would not classify myself in those years as a ballroom dancer.

My second wife, Susan, and I enjoyed dancing as well. We could hold our own in a fast dance contest, or in a hotel lounge, or disco, but again, I was not a ballroom dancer back then. After living in Florida a few years, a couple down the street, Margaret Ann and David, parents of kids who went to school with Susan's kids, talked to us casually about some lessons in ballroom dancing they were taking with a few other couples. They were going to a dance studio owned by Mary Dague, a local instructor in Lakeland, Florida, where we lived. David told me with a wink that dancing acts like an aphrodisiac and gets you both into a romantic mood. Sounded good to me, and while that probably wasn't the reason we joined in on those lessons—well, maybe it did influence me just a little—we did accept their invitation, and that's when my long, and happy excursion to become a ballroom dancer began. That was about twenty years ago. I wish now that I had begun this journey many, many years earlier. Actually, I'm still on the journey—I am a perennial student of dance, which is why I am trying to persuade you to do so at your earliest opportunity. At any age, though, it's never too late (nor too early) to take the first step to becoming a Man of Confi-Dance.

Susan and I took group classes for several years and joined the local USABDA (United States Amateur Ballroom Dancing Association) chapter and became active members—the name has since been changed to USA Dance. As our lessons and ability progressed, we moved on to a more challenging phase of ballroom dancing: competitions held by various USABDA chapters including our own chapter in Lakeland, in the greater Tampa Bay area.

Competing in ballroom dancing, even at the beginner's level, was daunting and reminded me of how I'd felt before a race when I competed in track years before. While it's tough on the nerves, the one thing you gain from competing is learning to focus. You focus completely on the steps and patterns you will perform until muscle memory kicks in, but the bottom line is that you come away with some nice steps and patterns that will perhaps stay with you forever. We competed at the beginner's level first, then the bronze level for a while, moving into a few silver level competitions too. As you get better, so does the competition, but in the end it was probably well worth the effort just for the experience, and I encourage each dancer to consider it in your area. There will be more about competition in Chapter 29.

Ironically, Margaret Ann and David, the couple who started us taking lessons, along with Susan and me, eventually divorced. Yes, dancing may be romantic, but it makes no guarantees. Margaret Ann continued to live a couple of blocks down the street from me, and from time to time when I might be working in my yard or in my garage with the garage door open, she might pull into my driveway, jump out of her car, and shout, "Dance me around the driveway." So I would hum a waltz and dance her around the driveway for a couple of minutes; after which she would jump back into her car and continue on home. A Man of Confi-Dance's work, it would seem, is never done!

After our divorce, Susan and I continued to date exclusively for another three years attending dance functions whenever and wherever possible due to our partnership in dancing. And I would have to say that our dancing on a regular basis was a major romantic influence in our relationship continuing on as it did during these years.

As the chapter heading states, "Wives may come and go, but dancing never leaves you." In fact, the dancing ladies in your life don't have to be limited to wives, and these ladies may also come and go. When Susan moved on with her life after becoming involved with someone else she met in a basic swing class, dancing helped me keep in touch with other ladies. I continued attending dances and zeroed in on a particular lady I had noticed some nice vibes from when we'd danced in the preceding months. I invited this lady, Barbara Larson, to a dance, and within months we were dance partners, and within another year or so we were engaged. She had begun dancing when she was young—to American Bandstand in front of the TV in the living room. She would go out dancing with her sister maybe four nights a week—not ballroom—just whatever the kids at the time were dancing. "We had no structure in those days," Barbara had told me, "just freestyle."

When she moved to Florida, she became interested in ballroom dancing. "Between boredom and wanting a challenge, I began with country line dancing," she added. Mary Dague, my instructor, then introduced her to ballroom dancing. Her first partner was Gene Tucci, whom I will introduce to you in more detail later, in '97. My Lakeland Sertoma club's Almost World Famous Sock Hop was her first big dance. She says, "I still have dancing in my blood—I'm probably obsessed." Today, she has progressed in her training so much that she's now learning the man's part. This has given her a greater appreciation of what the men have to learn because they have to know more: how to lead, floor craft, good rhythm, etc. Dancing is, and has been, a major part of her life now.

She tells me, "Men of Confi-Dance do not apologize in advance about how they will dance with you, they just take over—they're confident. They are looser, enjoying it." Her high point in dancing now is being able to dance with a professional and follow as if she were almost his equal, being comfortable that she can follow. "I'll probably dance until I die" is her firm admission.

I thought I had found a perfect partner in Barbara: someone I was in love with and someone who was an absolutely great dance partner. We started taking private lessons as well as group lessons; we then competed in some USABDA competitions in and around our hometown, and I thought I couldn't be happier. But somehow, someway, what we had was not working for Barbara, and she felt she needed to move on. When this happened, I was at a low point in my life. I had a hard time going to dances where she would also be attending. I changed to a new dance instructor and a new set of dance friends. Dancing was still the best social venue I could imagine, and I made progress, but very slowly, from the depths of despair I had felt. You may no longer have the dancing lady in your life, but you can and will still have dancing in your life, and that was a very comforting and major help then in my getting through a very difficult time.

CHAPTER 6

And All I Have To Do Is
Dance With The Ladies?

"When someone blunders, we say that he makes a misstep.
Is it then not clear that all the ills of mankind, all the tragic
misfortunes that fill our history books, all the political blunders,
all the failures of the great leaders have arisen merely from the
lack of skill in dancing?"

—Moliere

SEVERAL MONTHS AFTER the split-up with my fiancée and dance partner, Barbara, I learned about a USABDA-sponsored cruise for ballroom dancers and that gentlemen dance hosts would be needed. I decided to inquire how I might become a dance host on this cruise. Elly Engberg, the lady that USABDA had contracted to take care of the dance hosts—gentlemen with good dancing experience who would dance with the unattached ladies in the group in exchange for a free cruise—was a travel agent in Tennessee. Her company was known as Let's Dance Cruises, specializing in promoting cruises for ballroom dancers. She already had a number of dance hosts that she used on her own company's cruises available to her, but it turned out she needed more. I applied, which required a letter from my dance instructor (Mary Dague) rating my level of competence in the various ballroom dances, a letter from our USABDA chapter president, a letter from a female chapter member, a picture of me dressed for dancing, and several other items.

RW with Elly Engberg of Let's Dance Cruises

I was accepted. And so began my second life as a gentleman dance host on cruises all over the world which has been going on since 2003. I go with several companies like Elly's such as Dancers at Sea and Dancing Over the 7 Seas. I have sailed into many exotic ports around the world in the Caribbean, the Mediterranean, the Baltic, the Orient, around South America's Cape Horn, Alaska, the West Coast, Hawaii, Canada, Israel, Egypt, the South Pacific, New Zealand, and Australia. And there are still many I'd like to see. As a Man of Confi-Dance, a new door had been opened to me, and I went through wide-eyed and bushy-tailed and never looked back. Follow me to some of the places around the world I never expected to ever visit. Being a Man of Confi-Dance has given me this unique and wonderful opportunity.

RW asking Little Mermaid for a dance in Copenhagen, Denmark

MOC at Sphinx in Egypt

RW on guard in Scandinavian city

MOC dancing in bar in Central America

RW looking for real estate in Thailand

Dance hosts and gang ashore in Marseilles, France

Dance host RW having his beer in Rome, Italy

MOC dances with camel near pyramid in Egypt

RW taking dance cruise friends for tour of St Thomas

RW, in dance shirt, having beer with Joan Miller in Barcelona, Spain

RW, Nancy, Dean Cooke in wine country

RW, Dieter, and group in Quebec

Hamming it up with Dean, Tom, Howard, and ladies

RW, Tom, and Dean in Istanbul

RW with Wendy, aka Shakira, in Egypt

RW with Joan Miller at Peterhof Castle in Russia

RW with Bernie, Joan, and Gillian in Beijing, China

And all I have to do is dance with the ladies! That's right. I like to kid that my dance lessons finally paid off, but it is really true. While it does take being a good dancer to become a dance host on cruise ships, it takes more than dancing ability to keep you as a dance host.

RW with Trish on formal night

I have made many friends from all over our great country, and from a few other countries as well, from among my fellow dance hosts, and from among the many ladies I have danced with while out to sea. I have recently become engaged with a wonderful lady from Greenville, South Carolina, Nancy McMillon, whom I met initially on a cruise to Alaska and, surprisingly, again almost three years later in the airport in Tahiti waiting to board a ship where she was to be in the group of ladies I would be dancing with throughout the South Pacific and the Hawaiian Islands. As I will recount later, Nancy and I met and

Raoul and Nancy dressed to the nines

then parted. And later found the warm healing waters of Bora Bora to be a wonderful place to reconnect with a lady I cared about several years before. My dancing allowed this fateful opportunity to take place.

The Man of Confi-Dance has an endless supply of doors and windows that can open to him: the places he can go, the people he can meet, the travel he can enjoy, and the lifestyle he can lead—because he is a Man of Confi-Dance. As it did for me, dancing can keep you active socially during the times in your life when you may be without a significant other. You don't have to use dancing as a way to connect with women, but dance venues certainly place you in a position to meet ladies with the same interests perhaps faster than most other social activities.

MOC sitting at dinner with ladies on cruise;

RAOUL WEINSTEIN

MOC doing Elvis with Elvis on cruise

CHAPTER 7

The Young And The Innocent

"To learn to dance by practicing dancing or to learn to
live by practicing living, the principles are the same."
—Martha Graham

WHILE MOST MEN know and understand what self-esteem is and roughly how high or low their individual level runs, we might possibly forget that young boys face the same challenges to their level of confidence too.

A short while back I was asked to judge a ballroom dance contest. I thought, *This means I've come a long way in dancing to be invited to be a judge at a competition.* Then I learned I would be judging fifth graders! Dreams of fancy ladies in exquisite gowns swirling around the dance floor had to be pushed out of my mind.

I was told to be at the Highlands Grove Elementary school in Lakeland, Florida, by 9:00 a.m. and check in at the office. It was the final day of a six-week session of teaching fifth graders swing, waltz, and rumba by a close and longtime dance friend of mine, Linda Stata Pelton, who was completing her third year as a volunteer teaching these youngsters not only dance, but the graces of interacting with the opposite sex in a polite and respectful manner. I was delighted to participate and to observe these young students overcoming their fear, behaving like young gentlemen and ladies, and showing those who were in attendance what they had learned.

Each boy picked a dance (swing, waltz, or rumba) from slips of paper in a bag, and then picked the name of one of the girls from another bag, and would then proceed to walk over to this young lady and politely invite her to dance with him. After the dance, he was to walk her back to her seat. Linda would help each boy get started on beat as the music began, and two other judges, and I would hold up our numbers just like the judges on *Dancing with the Stars* and applaud their efforts.

"Learning how to interact with each other is a social skill they can use for the rest of their life," Linda explains. "At the beginning of each session, the kids are reluctant, even afraid of touching each other, but once they get started, they love it for the most part." She does this six-week program with each of the fifth-grade classes at the school on their PE period once or twice a week. She began this when her two granddaughters were in the second grade at the school to show them what community service is like. She also secretly hoped they would like to take up dancing and like it as much as she does.

Linda Stata Pelton with kids at competition finale

I talked to the boys who came in first, second, and third in the competition. The first place finisher was Austin Benjamin Smith, twelve, smiling at his accomplishment as he told me, "This is my first time dancing and I think it's awesome." I asked him what he liked most about the dancing he had learned. "I like the movements, I like that you don't just stand still, and I get excited and enjoy it," he replied. "And the girls—it's fun dancing with them—I thought it would be." Austin, you've just caught on to one of the most beneficial things you can learn about girls while you are young enough in life to enjoy it for many years.

Second place finisher, Zane Lundsford, also admitted this was his first time, and he also liked it. He didn't think he would in the beginning and was somewhat afraid. "But it's different now," Zane states. "It was easier than I thought it would be. Girls like dancing with the boys who are better." Welcome home, Zane, and keep up that attitude and your new level of confidence.

In third place, though really just as smooth as the other two, was Benjamin Royce Estridge, just ten years old, who indicated he had no prior experience dancing either. He also wasn't sure that he would like it, like most of the other boys. Was he afraid to try? "Not really," Ben told me. I saw him saying something earlier to his partner in the finals and now asked him what he was discussing with her. "I told my partner to smile because we would get bonus points," he said. Ben is already smart enough to know how to get ahead in a competition. I just hope all three of these polite young gentlemen continue in the field of dancing. It will enhance their relationships with girls for many years to come and always be a source of self-esteem.

I watched Linda work with the kids, reviewing with them for a few minutes before the competition began. She reminded the boys to invite and escort the girls back to their seats after the dance, and asked them some general questions about ballroom dancing that she had taught them over the past five weeks. It became clear to me how dedicated she is to this noble endeavor. It further increased my respect for a fellow dancer I already admire for her ongoing efforts and perseverance in getting many of us dancers together for events, parties, openings, or any opportunity for us to do some fun dancing. So let's spend a few moments right now and meet Linda Stata Pelton, fifty-nine, a longtime resident of Lakeland, and a dance friend of mine for close to twenty years.

Dancing came into her life in the fall of '91, when her husband (at the time) had gone off on an extended hunting trip, and she was left home alone with nothing to do. She took a group lesson at Kelly Recreation Center. Once she began these lessons, it was like putting her toe into the water, and she slowly inched her way into it. She was very precise in trying to keep it in moderation, took a weekly class, and attended the monthly USABDA dance.

"Early in my life, I was doing mostly nonfeminine sports like shotgun sports, motorcycle racing, tournament water skiing—I was a real tomboy," she recalled. "I never had the confidence as a girl to dance, not like the pretty girls, feeling more like the tomboy I was. As a youngster, I was an outsider, a wallflower, and no one asked me to dance. So I guess I didn't really miss it. But over the years, dance has meant a lot." Once divorced, she found a group of terrific dance friends, and for the first time she felt feminine, attractive, and enjoyed real male attention. Men invited her to dance and gave her compliments for the first time.

I see and know her as confident in asking guys to dance now. All of us know her standard line when meeting a new guy at a dance venue: "Hi, I'm 'Leenda,' would you like to rumba?" And Leenda does rumba a lot. "Social dancing is a safe environment, and if a lady invites a gentleman to dance, she has no fear of being rejected," she says with a smile. "And most men do accept. It's not the same as in a lounge or bar situation where guys just might have a different agenda."

Why does she enjoy helping others to dance so much? "I think back to being a wallflower in junior high and want young people to learn how not to be on the outside" is Linda's answer. She gets people involved and part of the group. She wants them to be happy. She is always willing to show others what she knows. At Highland Grove Elementary school, she went to the principal and pitched the idea of having a ballroom dance class for fifth graders during PE period. She loves it, and the kids get much from it too including learning social graces. She tells the girls that "when a boy invites you to dance, you accept—remember it's two minutes out of your life, it is not a marriage proposal." Years ago, she began a group as part of the outreach program from our local USABDA chapter for several semesters at Florida Southern College in Lakeland. In fact, one couple from that original group began competing, then got married, and even considered turning professional.

Linda says she just loves Men of Confi-Dance, and even if they are not necessarily the best dancers, she's always thrilled to be asked to dance and always gets something from it. "Dancing with a large circle of gentlemen is rewarding," she points out, "and you are not limited to just those few steps your regular partner or significant other knows. Dancing is probably one of the best social outlets you can find—you can use it your entire life unlike many other hobbies and sports."

Another member of our USA Dance chapter assists Linda with these fifth graders at Highlands Grove Elementary. Konstantin "Dino" Dedes, sixty-six, was born in Greece but grew up in the USA, "the best country in the world," he says. Dino provides the adult male figure in these classes and helps "keep the boys in line" when and as needed. He helps demonstrate the boy's steps with Linda in class. I asked Dino if he remembered the time when he couldn't dance, but his reply was, "I always knew how to dance—I have feelings and passion that makes a difference between me and others. And these are more important than lessons."

I jokingly refer to Dino as the local Lounge Lizard because he is well-known around here in most of the lounges and bars where he can dance with the ladies. In this element, with some ballroom dance lessons over the years under his belt, Dino is a Man of Confi-Dance. He has the knack of making ladies happy there. He describes his dancing as "having depths of joy and passion, and every lady says I give her happiness, and people watching tell me I bring them joy when I dance." Dino has taken what he needs from ballroom dancing and stamped it with his personal passion and joy to make his partners enjoy dancing with him as well as any other Man of Confi-Dance. Ladies tell him that they wish their husbands, or fiancés, or boyfriends would dance like he dances with them.

"There is a spiritual joy in dancing that is profound, unknown to people who don't know how to dance," Dino says. Perhaps it is his Greek heritage, like Zorba, the Greek. He loves the tango because of its passion, plus the waltz, and in Latin dances he enjoys the salsa and cha cha mostly. He believes, "Men who don't dance are missing everything in life—like a gardenia without fragrance, or like a church without icons. Dancing brings you joy, makes you live." Quite profound, Dino, but it sure makes the point for dancing, doesn't it?

Two weeks after judging this group of fifth graders, I was back at Highland Grove Elementary as part of a panel of five judges for the final competition of the entire fifth grade. This time there was quite an audience. Everyone in the fifth grade who was not participating in the competition, as well as many of the parents and siblings of those who were, including many of the teachers and staff members. It was a big moment for many of these youngsters. I was proud to be part of this event.

One of my fellow judges was Kevin Rios, thirty-three, one of the owners and instructors of Just Dance, a dance studio in Lakeland. When he gave out some certificates for free lessons as part of a Junior Ballroom program to the winners, I asked him about this program. He told me, "It's a new program promoting ballroom dancing to kids of all ages; we have kids from four to fifteen or sixteen. We focus on all of the different dances, and we show how ballroom dancing promotes respect, manners, and basic etiquette that kids will need throughout life. The boys learn how to ask a girl to dance, escort her back after the dance, and the basic social innuendos." Kevin feels that the more you instill at an earlier age the easier it will be when they are older. Many of his older students lament that they didn't learn this earlier. Hey, I'm still lamenting this myself!

His dance background began in Louisiana, at around nineteen or twenty, with no experience at all, weighing about three hundred pounds, heavy, awkward, and never before having touched a dance floor. He was truly an outsider when it came to dancing. He answered an ad to be trained to teach dancing. "I tried to hang on for the thirteen weeks at this Arthur Murray studio," Kevin told me, "with training from 4:00 to 9:00 p.m., and got trained for free. By the end, three other girls and I were the only ones who graduated. And I've been at it ever since, it's my main livelihood." Kevin Rios, now a true Man of Confi-Dance, is always volunteering in the community in any way he can to help promote dancing. Teaching kids at an early age is certainly a wonderful way to spread the joy of dancing—for many, many good years ahead.

As ballroom dancing continues its rise in popularity around the country, I would believe that there are many such programs available for the "young and the innocent" sponsored or aided by experienced ballroom dancers. They might be outreach programs from local dance chapters, colleges, recreation programs, or the like. It's a wonderful opportunity to have young boys and girls learn the basics of ballroom dancing, an option that I sorrowfully passed up early in my life. I encourage anyone reading this book that has influence over kids of the right age to dance to seek out these opportunities in your communities. One day, a Man of Confi-Dance (or a very happy lady with a man in her life who loves to dance with her) may thank you for what you helped bring into their lives many years before.

Section Two

HAPPINESS
Live Better, Live Longer

I HAVE SAID AGAIN and again that happiness is one of the world's most elusive commodities—you can't make it, you can't buy it, you can't will it; you just have to wait until it comes to you. But you can do a number of things that just might make happiness stay with you longer, or come calling faster. When one is happy, one will live far better and hopefully live longer.

Most of us are happiest when we have a sense of self-worth, a sense of well-being with a partner in life, and a sense of accomplishment in the things we do. In my life, being able to dance confidently has brought me much happiness. Studies have shown that ballroom dancing is one of the best activities as you get older for a healthy mind as well as a healthy heart. It is a social activity with many benefits. It may be a wonderful source of keeping a current relationship strong or a way to find and develop a new one. You will meet several Men of Confi-Dance throughout this book, and their level of self-respect and happiness is usually apparent. Besides, they seem happy, and they make many women happy.

CHAPTER 8

Okay, Maybe It's Dancing With One Special Lady

"Dancing is about being exactly who you
want to be in that moment."
—Katey Miller (Romola Garai),
Dirty Dancing: Havana Nights (2004)

YOU MIGHT BE thinking right now that because you are married, tied down to a demanding job, have kids not out of school yet, or no spare time to do anything, that none of this pertains to you. Okay, so maybe you won't become a dance host (maybe not right now), maybe you won't travel to exotic ports of call, or maybe you won't sweep the ladies off their feet every time you show up at a dance. But being a Man of Confi-Dance still can have its place for many men—men perhaps just like you.

Is there a special lady in your life who will want you to dance with her perhaps for a unique event or special moment in time? For example, a wedding or an anniversary celebration, a major black tie event, a cotillion, or some other gala? Will you oblige her? Or will you disappoint her again? How often has your wife or significant other asked you to dance with her to some romantic song at a small night club where you've taken her for her birthday or your anniversary? And you just backed off with the same old excuse that you've hidden behind for years: "I don't know how to dance."

Or maybe you acquiesced and begrudgingly went out on the dance floor with her, held her and sort of shifted weight from one foot to the other in, or perhaps, out of time with the music, just to be a nice guy or to avoid a fight. And as soon as the song was over, you were out of there looking around hoping that no one was looking at you especially anyone you knew.

How was that for your partner? What could have been the highlight of the evening for her may have just been another depressing moment in her life as she realized this guy she married is never going to give her what so many women want on the dance floor: a dance she can enjoy, a dance she can be proud to be a partner to, a dance that will excite her and bring back memories of her earlier years, a dance that makes her smile, a dance that inspires her to look around the room to see who's watching her, wishing they could be having a dance like that, and who knows, maybe wishing they could be her. Bottom line: Could this woman be made happier?

There is a scene from the recent movie *Date Night*, with Steve Carrel and Tina Fey. Tina Fey, Steve Carrel's wife, is talking to one of her best friends who is breaking up with her husband. Her friend is talking about how mundane their life had become, and that now they just seem to be at best good roommates. She asks Fey's character, "When is the last time your husband danced with you?" Fey pauses for a moment and then laughs (without smiling) when she replies, "Probably at our wedding." Sad statement on a marriage, isn't it? Can this be you too?

Maybe there is a lady you'd like to have in your life, but you lack the confidence to make this happen. If you don't have a specific lady in mind, maybe you'd like to think you have what it takes to meet new ladies and find the right one for you. A man doesn't have to become an expert dancer to be a Man of Confi-Dance. He can be a Man of Confi-Dance as it applies to the situation, even if just a single or special situation. A man who has never exhibited an interest in, or a talent for, dancing may be confronted with a request from his daughter or his wife that he dance with one or both of them at his daughter's upcoming wedding. *Oh no!* But break it down and realize that this may be just one single dance. Is that going to kill you, to learn how to do one dance, to dance the one dance that will make your daughter happy, or your wife happy, on one of the most important days of your lives?

Most dance instructors will welcome your request to teach you how to do a simple waltz or even something easier that will get you through the evening's assignment. Some are available without your having to sign your life away for months of lessons. So go with your daughter or with your wife, and with just a few lessons (but with practice between lessons right up to the big day), you can become a Man of Confi-Dance for that specific dance on that specific day. On that day, and for that dance, you can take your daughter or wife confidently into your arms, go through the steps or patterns that you have been practicing for weeks, smile to the audience, smile to your daughter or wife, and smile to yourself, as you perform in front of your family and friends while the video camera is rolling. It might just be the highlight of your day, almost certainly it will be for their day, and the highlight of the wedding video for years and years to come.

In a recent Sunday newspaper magazine section, CitiFinancial ran a one-page ad announcing it is now OneMain Financial with a wonderful picture of a father dancing with his daughter at a wedding. Any father looking at this picture and seeing the smiles on both faces, not to mention the admiring looks of the wedding guests watching, would be missing out on one of the most warming and wonderful moments he could bring into his and his daughter's life if he were to refuse her request to dance with her at her wedding simply because he doesn't want to. The logo used with this picture uses the words: Your needs. Your goals. Your dreams. The picture says it all. Her dreams should be your needs and goals. Her happiness will be your happiness. Find a way to make her happy. Be the Man of Confi-Dance for that one special moment.

Even if your feet never touch the dance floor again after that day, even if you head straight for the bar for a stiff drink, you will have been a Man of Confi-Dance when it counted for your daughter, and/or for your wife, and if the truth be known, for yourself too. Family and friends who have never witnessed your ever being within two zip codes of a dance floor in your entire life will look at you with new respect—respect that a Man of Confi-Dance earns and deserves. At that moment, looking at everyone, looking at your daughter's face, and/or your wife's face, you will know that it was worth the effort.

Perhaps later, when for only the one hundredth time that day, when your wife thanks you for your wonderful contribution to making the day so special for her and snuggles up to you and says something like, "Why don't we take some more lessons, maybe learn the rumba, or the tango—that's such a romantic dance." *Listen to her!* Listen to and look for the new doors and windows that are ready to open to you—listen up and don't refuse out of habit. The new you, the new Man of Confi-Dance (albeit for only one dance) might be on the verge of breaking out into a new dimension, a new talent, a new persona, and finding the joys, benefits, and happiness that other Men of Confi-Dance have found.

Or perhaps you are seventeen years old and have been invited by one of the cutest girls at your school to be her escort at her cotillion or debutante ball, complete with a formal outfit and corsage and all the social hoopla that goes along with it. After you accept, beaming with pride, surprised that she'd pick you, and knowing the other guys will be jealous, you find out the down and dirty truth: You will be required to do a waltz, in turn as each of the other couples will have to do, where you will be on the dance floor only with her for a whole ninety seconds. Perhaps the longest minute and thirty seconds of your entire life so far because you don't know how to waltz!

It's too late now to back out. And what would she think of you if you tried? Young man, you too can become a Man of Confi-Dance for that specific dance on that specific day for that specific young lady. It means taking lessons (there might be someone on the organizing committee whose job it is to teach everyone how to waltz) with a qualified instructor. Yes, it may take some time and some effort on your part to adopt the right attitude (you had to do this to become the district two-hundred-meter champ this spring or the leading pass receiver last fall, didn't you?) and buckle down to the task at hand. If you're thinking that your buddies, the ones who weren't invited to escort any of these lovely young ladies, will be teasing you and making fun of you for having to do the waltz at the debutante ball, don't let it rattle you. Your reward will be far greater. When you finish taking that cute young lady out for a spin around the dance floor, you in your great-looking tuxedo, she in her elegant formal gown adorned by the beautiful corsage you gave her and long gloves, gliding through the waltz with a new Man of Confi-Dance, her radiant and dazzling smile, and her squeeze of your hand when you finish will make it all worthwhile. If there was any reason why she invited you to escort her in the first place, like maybe she has some interest in you, you can bet your rating with her just went off the scale.

And with the junior-senior prom coming up, you might find that there's no one else you'd rather take and that the waltz, which may not be on the playlists of any serious rock band playing at the prom, might lead you to rethink taking some more lessons in what will be the type of dancing that will go on that night. You might find that she can help with the current dances, or some friends might help, or as stated above, dance instructors who know all the latest dances can help you. This can be the new you moment in your life and serve you extremely well, not just right now, but for many years to come. You'll find happiness making her happy.

CHAPTER 9

A Specific Example Of One
Specific Dance

"Love is a lot like dancing—you just surrender to the music."
—Anonymous

A S STATED IN the definition given earlier of a Man of Confi-Dance, you might need to or want to be a Man of Confi-Dance for one specific dance for one specific reason. Whether that is the last time you are a Man of Confi-Dance or just the first time in a lifetime of being a Man of Confi-Dance remains to be seen. So let's take a look at one recent example.

This past year, my nephew, Jacob, who shares my birth date—we are two of the Men of June 10, got married at a very elegant and upscale wedding in Nashville, Tennessee. It was a wonderful affair with excellent food, drinks, and a great band that could play any type of music requested. Nancy and I attended and had a ball. But the highlight for me was when Jacob and his new wife, Ali, began their first dance.

Months before, Nancy and I offered to teach Jacob and Ali some dance steps for their first dance as a married couple. When they came over from Tampa to Lakeland for dinner and a lesson in my dance room, it was apparent that while they each had rhythm and a good ear for music, neither had any structured dancing experience—at least no formal ballroom dancing experience. When they told us what song they wanted to use, we decided to demonstrate some moves from a new niche dance called the Night Club Two Step. The NC2S works well for slower songs to which no other ballroom dance fits properly. But it was a good dance for the song they selected. We showed them some basics, how to add a few hot moves, and then showed them some basic rumba steps. They enjoyed the lesson, really got into it, and promised they would practice, and hopefully come back another time before the wedding for some additional instruction.

Well, that was their only lesson, and when they came out on the dance floor for their first dance as man and wife, I held my breath. As the slow sultry notes of their song—they chose Etta James's beautiful and soulful, *At Last*—began, they circled each other on the dance floor (as we had suggested) then came together into some basic NC2S steps moving right to the music with some drops and sways (looked like something from one of the rumba steps we practiced, but changed to fit their style), and some things that they had added. But watching them dance, the one thing that stood out to me was that whatever they had choreographed from what we had shown them, Jacob looked like the leader, he looked like he was in control, and it was beautiful and sensuous to watch. The Jacob that led that dance at that moment was a Man of Confi-Dance in my eyes.

Instant MOC Jacob and bride Ali at wedding

And I'm quite sure in Ali's eyes too, and it wouldn't surprise me if that wasn't true in the eyes of most of the other ladies watching. I didn't see them dancing much more that night because they were making the rounds greeting and hugging everyone in that large reception room. I still don't know if they can dance anything else, but during the dance that counted, the dance that will probably be remembered for years to come, they had it, and he had it. From the applause they received, more than polite patting of hands together, a Man of Confi-Dance was born that night.

CHAPTER 10

Here I Am, Show Me How It's Done

"Any problem in the world can be solved by dancing."
—James Brown

FOR A MAN, ballroom dancing in particular, and other dancing to a great extent, is an area where you are in control. This may be the first time this is made clear, in front of you and your partner. If you are in a class, it will also be made clear in front of everyone that in each couple, there is only one leader (you, the man) and only one follower (your partner). This is very powerful and welcome news as it may very well be the first, and perhaps the only, time you will be in the lead in the partnership you are in.

Yes, you da man, you da man! She may tell you when you're going to eat dinner, and she may tell you what you are going to wear that night, and she may even tell you what night will be your lucky night, but you are going to tell her when she is going to step backward or forward, and when she is going to go under your raised arm, and when she is going to turn to her right or her left! Pretty cool, huh? You are going to be the leader, and she is going to be the follower, and you are on your way to becoming a Man of Confi-Dance.

This may not be happening in too many other areas of your married life! Just don't abuse it. It can be intimidating when you are new to dancing, especially if you find yourself dancing with someone other than your usual partner. But it is one of the best ways to get better and build your confidence. I remember when I was learning to ballroom dance, and we'd go over to the Rhapsody Ballroom near Tampa, a really nice ballroom to enjoy some midweek dancing. They would always have a mixer or two where the ladies would line up on one side of the dance floor, and the men would come down the line taking the lady at the head of the line for a turn around the floor, depositing her at the end of the line, and then taking the next lady at the front of the line around the floor. Talk about intimidation—worrying that I could lead those long-legged, long-stepping Tampa ladies through the waltz or foxtrot. But it was definitely a learning experience, and one that I still recall when I hear a guy verbalize his fear about leading a lady who is a better dancer. You will find most partners very patient. After all, everyone on the floor was a beginner once upon a time.

So maybe you are now thinking that you might like to be da man, and you would therefore be interested in learning to dance, perhaps for one of the following reasons:

1. Your daughter wants you to dance with her at her upcoming wedding?
2. Your wife wants you to dance with her on your anniversary? Or you are the wife, and you want your husband to dance with you on your anniversary?
3. Your new girlfriend thinks it would be *cool* to learn the Argentine tango?
4. There's a dance after the football game next week, and that cute girl in your algebra class asked if you were going to be there, and you don't want to be embarrassed when she finds out you can't dance?
5. Your best friends have told you about all of the women at a local dance club, and you don't know how to dance well enough to even ask a lady to dance? Or you are a woman, and your friends have told you that there are all kinds of guys at a local dance club but you don't know how to dance?
6. You find yourself single again and don't know how to get back into the dating scene?
7. You know a little about dancing but not enough to feel confident going to a dance?
8. You've been watching *Dancing with the Stars* and think you'd like to be a pro and dance with a star like Pamela Anderson, or you are a woman and think you'd like to dance with the pro Maks Chmerkovskiy?
9. You've read that ballroom dancing is one of the best activities for senior citizens to stay mentally and physically alert?
10. The friends you associate with socially are taking dance lessons and invited you and your significant other to join them?
11. Something I've said earlier in this book has shown you a reason or two for being a Man of Confi-Dance, and you're ready to start reaping some of those benefits?

If you are a man reading this and would like or need to consider learning to dance, there are many options. If you are a woman reading this and would like to think that you could convince your boyfriend or husband or significant other to learn to dance, the same things apply.

There are various options for taking dance lessons. Probably the most obvious method of learning to dance is to take dance lessons from a professional dance instructor. That is how I learned almost all of what I know about dancing and what the majority of novices will do, and it's what you should do in most cases. You may have a friend or relative who is willing to teach you some dance steps. You may have a significant other who can teach you to dance. You may be good enough to pick up dancing from observing others at a dance venue or from a DVD on ballroom dance lessons. But most of you should, and hopefully will, take from a pro.

In 1966, in one of their big hits, The Association sang something like, "And then along comes Mary." My pro for the majority of training in ballroom dancing was Mary Dague in Lakeland, Florida, my hometown for many years. So let's meet Mary, fifty-eight, dance instructor and the owner of Dancin', A Ballroom Society in Lakeland, a teacher for twenty-one years at her studio and at the city-owned Kelly Recreation Center. She is married to Bill, her second husband, who ably assists her in many of her classes. Mary told me, "I have always been somewhat obsessive about ballroom dancing and can't seem to get it out of my system yet."

Mary and Bill Dague at her studio

RAOUL WEINSTEIN

Earlier Mary taught for some independent studios in the area until opening her own. When I asked about her early dancing, she told me she had been a baby crib rocker and as a child would put on dance shows for her friends, all without the help of any dance lessons. "I went to all the sock hops in school and wanted to be a go-go girl, but my history teacher told me I was much too smart to be a go-go girl. So I tried nursing, I was a horticulturist, a travel agent, but nothing seemed to fit. Then I began taking ballroom lessons with my first husband in Pennsylvania, but he wasn't very good, and it wasn't that much fun," she says. After they divorced, she married Bill, whom she said had a real fear of dancing, but she talked him into going for lessons. They were both nervous about it, running late, but they did take the class and completed the basic course, plus another one.

Then she saw Patrick Swayze in *Dirty Dancing* and dreamed of dancing with him. Swayze became her inspiration for ballroom dancing; she even named her dog Swayze. In fact, one of the highlights of their dance life according to Mary was when Mary and Bill and some of the dancers from her studio performed the ending scene from *Dirty Dancing* at one of our Lakeland Sertoma Club's annual Almost World Famous Sock Hops.

Mary has been teaching for a long time at Kelly Recreation Center in Lakeland—group lessons that are affordable for people to learn the basics, so they can decide if they want to continue. She's happy to teach couples and singles how to dance, but she's not in it just to sell dance lessons—she loves it, loves her job (likes to make money), but loves to have people learn and love to dance. She does not require a contract like most studios, which is very admirable and takes the fear away for newcomers. She uses her studio to help people for their specific needs such as weddings, often choreographing some little routines for the bride and groom. Another need she helps people with is preparing them to dance at class reunions (usually the swing). Mary feels *Dancing with the Stars* has had a major impact on lessons and a renewed interest in dancing. "My classes have been full for the last six years, with a waiting list," she says.

We talked about being a Man of Confi-Dance. Mary says, "He does not necessarily have to be able to dance with everyone but just dancing with his partner, his wife, his girlfriend. If he can get out in a strange situation, in front of strangers, and can dance, he's then a Man of Confi-Dance. Hearing music and going out and dancing with or without others dancing on the floor, there's a Man of Confi-Dance. He can bring joy and happiness into his lady's life."

Good answer, Mary!

She further advises, "Many of the people who come to beginners lessons are impatient—you won't be a good dancer in two lessons. Ladies have to be patient with their partners—don't give up or get bored. The man's job is much more difficult but has much more power. He can be the musical force—in charge of the music. Don't compare yourself too much with other people; it's okay to look at others and say, 'I'd like to dance like that,' but don't expect it quickly, and don't think that you are not as good when you compare yourself with them because practice can make that happen. Don't worry about what other dancers are seeing you do; they are into what they are doing. And ladies, have fortitude," she says. "Have perseverance with your dance lessons. You can have a bad night with your partner. Just close your eyes and go with the music and don't give up."

As mentioned earlier, when I was married to Susan, we were invited by some friends in our neighborhood to join them along with other couples for some group lessons at Mary's studio. Remember, I had always loved to dance from the time I was born at the age of fifteen. The dancing I had always enjoyed through the years was what my peers at the time (high school and college) were doing. And for all the intervening years, that's what I still danced, with perhaps the addition of a little chalypso and some niche or fad dances like the twist, the frug, the stroll, etc.

So when Susan and I (we even had a few fast dance contest wins over the years under our belts) began taking beginner ballroom dance lessons, I thought it would be a piece of cake. It turns out that my fast dance expertise had to be relearned as the triple—or single-step swing, and thus it took me a good while to get into the new mode of fast dancing. But learning basic ballroom dances that were new to me like the waltz, foxtrot, rumba, and tango went well. The cha cha was much the same as the basic chalypso learned years ago but now more structured.

We enjoyed learning to ballroom dance correctly for the first time in our lives and found out quickly that if you don't practice what you learn between lessons, you quickly lose it. Mary had the answer to this, of course: join her Friday night social dance party where you pay a lump sum in advance for either a six-month or a twelve-month membership, and you then come to her studio every Friday night for ballroom dancing. And so we became Friday night regulars, and ballroom dancing became an enjoyable and structured part of our lives. There were other dancers to watch who were more advanced, and there were beginners not far behind us who motivated us to practice to stay ahead. We became friends with one guy who was more advanced, along with his wife. He would always dance at least one dance with almost every lady there on a Friday night to be social and to make sure they all had the opportunity to dance. The wife of the couple who originally got us into taking lessons, Margaret Ann, sat back down near us one Friday night after dancing with this advanced dancer and made the following comment, "Wow, that dance with him might just be better than sex!"

Now that sounds like a mighty profound compliment. Makes one think that dancing must really make her happy!

CHAPTER 11

Join The Group—There's Safety (And Savings) In Numbers

"Dancing can reveal all the mystery that music conceals."
—Charles Baudelaire

M ANY COMMUNITIES HAVE recreation centers that schedule classes for many different activities, including ballroom dancing. Group lessons can be very reasonable in price, and I would suggest that you check out the situation in your town. In Lakeland, Florida, ballroom dance lessons were offered through our city recreation programs at one or more of the city recreation centers. Our center has an Olympic-sized pool, a gymnasium for basketball and volleyball, a complete fitness and weight room, steam rooms, and a wonderful large room with a great wooden floor perfect for aerobics and ballroom dance classes. Mary Dague was the pro the city contracted to teach the group classes. I took advantage of these for years, at an average of $3 or less per week for classes that ran anywhere from eight to sixteen weeks, where you can join with or without a partner.

When Susan and I originally began lessons with Mary, we were part of a small group, and basically we were splitting Mary's hourly rate for private lessons in her studio. But with group lessons, the groups could be large and thus more comfortable when you are a beginner and not that confident, but will not hinder one's opportunity to learn and improve. A session might include two to three weeks of waltz, two to three weeks of rumba, two to three weeks of tango, and two to three weeks of swing for example. If you had to miss a week, the previous week's lesson was always reviewed at the beginning of each week's class until it appeared most of us were okay with it, and then we moved on to either the next part of that pattern or a new pattern or a new dance. Even if you were to miss a few weeks in a row and miss out entirely on the foxtrot, for example, you could still benefit by the instruction in the other dances being taught during that session. While couples benefit most, singles are also welcome. Mary does her best to either pair singles up for the entire session or to make sure they are rotated in with the group enough to get the feel of either leading (men) or following (women).

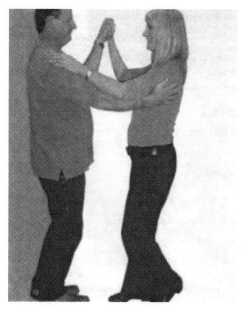

Mary Dague teaching dance student

I have seen couples begin these group lessons thinking they'll never make it through or amount to much on the dance floor, only to see them months later beginning to really look like dancers. I am constantly surprised by the progress made by couples who will stick with it, attend the classes with a good attitude, and find the time to practice at home what they've learned each week. If you don't practice the lessons, the patterns, the steps, the form that you've been learning, you will be wasting your time and money. Find time at home to practice dancing, find places to go where you can dance to review what you are learning, join dance groups in your area, find out where dancing is being offered, and you will progress quickly, you will enjoy it, and you will feel a sense of accomplishment.

After taking the beginner class, Susan and I would then sign up for the intermediate class—again and again and again, for it was different each time, with new tips on framing, or arm styling, or leading, or following, mixed with new patterns and steps to learn and master. At any time, Mary would certainly welcome any of her students to schedule private lessons.

They were reasonably priced and gave you the opportunity to work on something from group class, to learn something a little more advanced, perhaps be taught a showcase routine for some exhibition or prepare for some upcoming competition.

Over the past few years, my good dance friend, Donna Grogan, who lives and instructs dancers in the Brandon area between Lakeland and Tampa, has served a lot of us with the opportunity to take group lessons, workshops, private lessons, and then apply what we've learned at her monthly dances. Each dance usually has a theme and an exhibition by some of the really talented amateur and professional dancers from throughout the entire Tampa Bay area. On top of that, Donna also serves plenty of great food at each of her dances.

Donna with performers Walt and Jan Ward

Donna has invited me to be a DJ at her 50' and 60's dances where I bring my collection of 45's and spin those great songs on turntables for the dancing enjoyment of those attending. She and I have held several workshops teaching the Night Club Two Step, and it has always been a highlight of the night for me when we get out on the floor and do a NC2S or a West Coast swing in our unconventional and funky style, and I miss our dancing together now that I have relocated to South Carolina.

CHAPTER 12

Outsiders And Insiders—A Vast Difference

"A man who knows how to dance can make any woman feel good."

—Barbara Haller

I 'VE SAID IT before and I'll say it again: it is never too early in your life, nor ever too late in your life, to learn to dance. As long as people around you of your approximate age dance, whatever the dances are, it's a good time to be a participant. Be one of the gang if you can. Outsiders usually develop a feeling of being an outsider very quickly and find it a stigma they cannot remedy easily. And it can make you very unhappy. Insiders know when they are insiders. Become a Man of Confi-Dance, and you can generally sidestep being an outsider. I am an insider most of the time now that I can dance.

That being said, I will admit that being an insider most of the time does not necessarily guarantee that you won't find yourself on the outside from time to time. Some of these times of being an outsider took place well past the point where I became what I call a Man of Confi-Dance. You see, while you might consider yourself a good dancer, a dancer who can dance most dances well enough, you might find that there are niches where you are still an outsider. I have been there and will probably still face times when I will be an outsider on occasion when it comes to dancing.

For years I considered myself good at dancing the swing. Going back to high school and college and even through the years before I took up ballroom dancing, I could always hold my own in the swing—dances with a fast tempo. When I began taking ballroom dance lessons, I found that I had to relearn the swing. Ironically, the dance I knew best also happened to be a hybrid step, not the proper basic steps for the swing that are used in social ballroom dancing and ballroom dance competition. It took more than a year for me to get comfortable with the accepted ballroom dancing style for swing.

After a while, I learned that swing, as we call it in general, is also known more specifically as East Coast swing. It has the triple-step version as well as a single-step version, depending on the tempo. Well then comes along a dance known as the West Coast swing. You guessed it, it started in California like everything else, I think and spread east. It is danced to a tempo a tad bit slower than East Coast swing and is danced in a slot. It takes a little work to get used to it, and it is now one of my favorite dances where I enjoy just getting funky, creative, and spontaneous.

But before I learned to be a Man of Confi-Dance in the West Coast swing, I went over to Tampa one night with a friend to where the Tampa Bay Beach Boppers held their weekly dances. I watched helplessly as everyone was doing the West Coast swing. I knew right away that I was not a Man of Confi-Dance here and was afraid to ask any of the ladies to dance. When I observed one lady who had great moves, moves that I surmised she could put to good use doing the East Coast swing like I do, I got my nerve up, and when a song came on that I determined could be as good for East Coast swing as for West Coast swing, I asked her if she'd like to do the East Coast swing with me (a Man of Confi-Dance in EC swing). Her reply was, "Oh, sorry, I don't do East Coast swing," and she turned and looked for someone with whom to do West Coast swing to this song.

That stung, but it also taught me a lesson: When you can't do the dances that everyone seems to be doing, you are more than likely an outsider. And that comes with all the frustration and disappointment that outsiders feel.

Just a couple of years ago, I was visiting my friend, Dean Cooke, a fellow dancer who has been on many dance cruises where I have hosted. He lives in Charleston, South Carolina, and he was right on my way on a trip I was taking up the east coast. We stuffed ourselves on seafood at one of Charleston's restaurants, after which he took me out to a roadhouse bar where they specialized in dancing the shag, a fun dance indigenous to the Carolinas, especially South Carolina. Again, I found myself watching good dancers do the shag and nothing else, and realized, as memories flooded back into my head of the Beach Boppers West Coast swing night in Tampa years before, that I was an outsider again.

I had never learned the shag. Even though the shag incorporates a lot of basic swing moves, it has a style and grace all its own, and if you can't do it right, the ladies you ask to dance are not going to like it. And I knew that and not being a Man of Confi-Dance in the shag doomed me that night to just watching for an hour before we finished our beers and left, quite unfulfilled (though still very filled by the great seafood and beer!)

The Argentine tango is now a dance attracting a lot of attention. If you know how to do the tango American-style, and I do, or even International-style, you are still not an Argentine tango dancer. I have yet to watch an Argentine tango exhibition or showcase where the lady I was with, or ladies around me, didn't swoon and verbalize their desire to take up Argentine tango. The sexiness and intimacy of the dance is palpable. A man who can lead a lady through an Argentine tango with the right moves and command will appear to any observer to be the epitome of a Man of Confi-Dance without doubt! What's so neat is that even though he is the leader, she has a lot of flexibility too and can take the initiative at any time. It will still appear as if he is in control and will still be dramatic to watch, let alone if you were actually to be involved in the dance itself. With the Argentine tango, I am, alas, still an outsider.

Nancy, my fiancée and the lady in my life now, has repeatedly mentioned to me that she'd like for us to take lessons in Argentine tango. I know that the correct decision for me is to find the time to learn this dance with her. Practice will be hard to keep up without the dance room I had in my Lakeland home, as we live in Greenville, South Carolina now and could be used as a valid excuse to forget this idea, but I am trying to improve on one of my weakest areas—listening to the lady in my life. So I am working on that and hopefully before too long I will no longer be an outsider but a Man of Confi-Dance in the Argentine tango. And making Nancy happy is a good thing, right?

I used to know some country and western dance steps and even went out to the dance places that catered strictly to that type of dancing. But I've lost what I had learned over the years from sheer lack of doing it much and will rarely go onto the dance floor to do that type of dancing when it's being played. I'm back to being an outsider when it comes to that style of dancing. But recently I was made aware that my sister, Karen, and brother-in-law, Bill Witte, met through their mutual interest in country and western dancing when they were both single again, living in the Maryland suburbs of Washington DC.

My sister Karen with Bill

Bill, now seventy-three, tells me he was a Man of Confi-Dance at the time they met while country and western dancing and that dancing was something that always made him feel good about himself even when he might be down otherwise. He felt in control when he was dancing even when he might not be in control of his life. He has known how to dance since learning in Florida at the age of twenty-three, mostly jitterbug, cha cha, and the current fads. Karen always loved to jitterbug in high school (she once beat me in a jitterbug contest with my own fraternity brother, Eddie Cohen, as her partner. I still can't seem to believe that really happened, Eddie) and loved dancing whatever was in fashion. In her forties, divorced, relatively new to Maryland, she was going to all the singles dances she could find when disco was big. Then she learned country and western, got into a crowd of dancers and was out dancing several nights a week. One night, this dude named Bill asked her to dance; they hit it off, laughed a lot, and after a few months of mostly country and western dance dates, they decided they wanted to be together. The initial attraction was dancing.

When they got married, dancing was a big part of their wedding celebration. They wanted to make it a party, so they had a country and western DJ and it made the evening.

Today? "We don't dance very much now," Bill told me. "But we love to dance at any event that offers dancing."

"We want to take some Latin lessons this summer," Karen added. "Dancing is still important to us." She smiled and finished by telling me she still sees Bill as a Man of Confi-Dance. Bill, you keep my sister happy now, you hear me?

CHAPTER 13

You Don't Have To Be A Boy Scout To "Be Prepared!"

**"Anyone who says sunshine brings happiness
has never danced in the rain."**

—Anonymous

I F YOU ARE in high school and want to learn hip-hop to be hip, find out from your peers how they learned. In most cases, it's probably learned from your friends or each other. Talk to them, ask them to teach you. Find a friend who won't tell the others that you don't know how to do the latest fad dances that others in your social group are doing. Often at parties, a song will be played and some of the gang will get up and start doing the latest craze. Watch them and then go home and practice.

I used to do that when I was in high school. The closet in my bedroom had two doors that opened out from the middle, each with a mirror on the inside. I could open and position those doors in a way that I could see my body from several angles as I tried to imitate the moves or gyrations I had seen others do at the latest dance or party. I would buy the music (45 rpm records in my day) and play them and work at doing what I had seen others do. I would try to do these steps or moves at the next party or dance and get to where I thought I was as good as anybody else. You can do something similar today. I had been a Boy Scout just a few short years before, but now I had a new reason for wanting to follow the old Boy Scout slogan: "Be prepared."

If you're a guy in his twenties or thirties working at a job in a new town where the local bars and roadhouses have country western dancing and you like drinking beer every Friday and Saturday night but don't know how to do the dances you watch from your barstool, what can you do to learn how to be as good as the next guy? I would bet that you have probably seen guys who are not as good-looking as you dancing with good-looking ladies you'd love to be dancing with. You might wonder how these guys are even talking to ladies who you'd think would have nothing to do with some of the guys they dance with. These guys may not be as handsome as you, may not dress as sharply as you, may not drive a pickup truck as cool as yours, may not make the money you make, but they are talking to and dancing with ladies that you are not talking to or dancing with. Am I right? They are giving these ladies what they want, at least what they want inside that bar where the music is playing and where guys like you are watching them strut their stuff.

Many bars that feature country and western dancing have classes before the evening gets going. Check it out, look for ads, listen to the country stations on the radio, and get with it. You might be surprised to find out that one of those good-looking ladies out there dancing would just melt at a guy like you asking them to help you learn to dance the way they like. They may even make it a personal project to help you, or they may point you in the right direction. But there will be places where you can learn those dances, and you can be the Man of Confi-Dance these high-stepping ladies want to dance with, be with, and perhaps end up with.

Perhaps you're a middle-aged guy who loves Latin music and wants to be adept at Latin dances like the salsa or an older guy who has recently lost a wife or significant other and wants to get back into the dating scene. Dancing, of whatever type that fits your lifestyle at that moment, might just be what will enhance your life and add a new and positive dimension. Whether it's hip-hop, country western, Latin, ballroom, or any other style of dancing that you see the guys that can do that particular dance well are in command, it's happening this way because each of these guys has become a Man of Confi-Dance for the style of dancing that goes on in that venue. It may be the only kind of dancing that they know, but it sure works for them, doesn't it? Maybe it's time you found out how to learn to do those dances too. Get started. And don't give up along the way because the rewards are well worth it.

It will quite likely take some time to become a Man of Confi-Dance in the dance you choose to learn (or learn more of), so "be prepared." A lot of people have grown up with the attitude that they can't dance. Unfortunately, men are usually the ones. Why? Perhaps they don't feel they have rhythm, and they aren't musically inclined and can't keep the beat. Or they tried at an early age and were embarrassed and never tried again. Maybe they had ladies in their lives that either couldn't dance themselves or didn't particularly have a desire to dance (possibly because they knew you couldn't dance). But this can be changed. Not everyone will become a great dancer, but many can learn enough to do an adequate job in the environment where it can serve them well and help them reap the many benefits. You don't have to be invited to perform on *Dancing with the Stars* to be acknowledged by most observers as a good dancer or even a Man of Confi-Dance.

Even if all you want or need is to learn just one dance for that special time in your daughter's life, or the right time to make your wife or significant other happy at an important event in her life, or maybe for some fundraiser where you are being pressured to perform a hot salsa with someone else in your company, there are pros that would teach and prep you enough to perform well even for that one dance. Call around and find one. I know dancers who started out needing to learn that one dance for that one event and then decided it would be fun to learn more. You can be a Man of Confi-Dance for that one dance, remember. Or you can be a Man of Confi-Dance for much more, maybe even for the rest of your life, if you so desire, or if someone important to you so desires. Keep her happy and you'll surely live longer because you will find that even just a *little* dancing with a lady will provide her with a *lot* of happiness.

To further my ambition to be prepared, whenever I am on a cruise as a dance host, and the instructor gives our group a lesson on our days at sea, I immediately go back to my cabin and make notes in my dance lessons notebook. It is not easy converting what you have just seen and demonstrated physically into words. There have been many times when I revisit those notes weeks, months, or years later to re-learn that particular step or pattern from some past cruise, only to find that the thirty lines of notes (with arrows, even) make absolutely no sense to me now. Words like "Then move Lady to my L keeping my R hd on her L shldr for the Q-Q and open her back on the next S, ending w/ Lady in cuddle pos . . ." What seemed so obvious to me as a way to describe some step that lasted all of four beats is now a complete mystery, probably never to be solved again. That's why practicing after every lesson is so important.

When I am at a dance where a complimentary lesson is being given, I always participate even when I am not there with a regular dance partner, which was most of the time when Nancy and I were living in two separate states. I have learned so many really nice steps or patterns that have since vanished from my mind that I have often said that I probably only do on a regular basis ten percent or less of the dance steps and patterns I have learned since I began dancing. My Lakeland friend, Gene Tucci, whom I've known for more than fifteen years through Mary Dague's Friday night dance group, group lessons, and our local dances, remembers every step and pattern he's ever learned, it seems. Whenever any of us is trying to recall how a particular pattern or step that we recently had in class is supposed to go, one of us will eventually sigh and yell out, "Let's ask Gino, he'll know."

Eugene Tucci, eighty-one, was born in Brooklyn and began dancing in Long Island in 1985, which he recalls as being a very slow process. After six months of private lessons, he went out and found he was still woefully lacking in both ability and confidence. The confidence came three or four years later with group lessons after work in NYC. He met a lot of women and guys, and they formed a group. Little by little, he gained the confidence he now has.

"When I was in the service," Gene told me, "I went to a USO party in Japan and watched guys having a good time dancing and vowed, 'One day I want to do that.'" Back then, he was the typical outsider watching the insiders having fun. Gene looks back and says that dancing has meant broadening his social outlook and adding confidence. He felt he was backward at one time, but dancing has helped bring him out. He gets a kick out of being with the friends he has met through dancing. And I have watched with admiration and much respect over the years Gene's willingness to ask every lady available to dance. His attitude is that, "Everybody wants to dance. You should give them that chance." His high point in dancing has been the compliments he's gotten from strangers when he's been at the top of his dance game on dance cruises with his friends. Gino is one of my favorite examples of a self-made Man of Confi-Dance.

Gino with Mary and Barb

At this point in my dancing, I analyze any new pattern or step I am learning in a group class as to whether or not I will be able to successfully lead a lady who was not at this class through what I have just learned. Even if I remember it exactly, some patterns cannot be led easily unless your partner has some idea of what you want her to do. So if she wasn't in the class with you, she may have no idea of what to do at some point in the pattern when you only have a one-hand lead, or she is now behind you, or has to do something that you can't lead. In the middle of some cool pattern, I have let go of the hands of ladies so they could go behind by back, never to set eyes on that lady again! Just kidding, of course, but when a lady is no longer under your control on the dance floor (as in life), there is no telling what she might decide to do, think she should be doing, or would like to do at that moment in the pattern. So you don't want to get too fancy with a lady you are dancing with for the first time until she is more comfortable with your lead, or you have had a chance to size her up a bit in terms of her prior training.

Once you learn to dance the style of dancing you desire, you will find your own happiness and sense of accomplishment in making the ladies around you happy on the dance floor. Life can be good. Life can actually be better. And you will have good reason to make sure you live longer!

Section Three

ROMANCE:
It Will Always Take Two to Tango

WHILE I CERTAINLY do not want to over-emphasize the role that dancing plays in romance, it's easy to recognize that of all the social activities in which men and women (often total strangers) partake dancing has to be one of the most intimate. Not only are you two holding hands, you have your arms on or around your partner, and your bodies are in close proximity and often touching. Sounds like the perfect recipe for romance to me.

For those of us involved in structured ballroom dance and members of dance clubs and groups, we dance with a number of partners other than our own wives or significant others. This is the courteous norm for social dancing and is harmless. But as we know not only from movies, television, and books, many a romance has either begun or has flared from the touching of two people in some dance position. It cannot be denied.

Where else can a guy go up to a perfect stranger in a lounge and use an innocent invitation to dance to gain the opportunity to meet a lady he admires that in any other circumstance he would have no good excuse to approach and even introduce himself? You won't know what to do with this alluring lady if you don't know how to dance. And let me also be very clear at this juncture: Ladies can easily resent a man coming into their space, holding them too tightly, making insinuating innuendos, and basically trying to put a move on them on the dance floor. This can be a complete turnoff to a lady who might very well have had an interest in you if you hadn't come on so strongly. In other words, dancing might be a great way to meet ladies, but it does not give a man unlimited license to abandon his manners and social graces.

But you can still go about the process of meeting ladies by being a gentleman with a lady you are dancing with and show a little class. It will go a long way in combination with your dancing skills to impress her if that's what you'd like to do. As I have alluded to earlier and will add to in the following chapters, I have had many romantic moments through dancing. Being a Man of Confi-Dance has provided these opportunities for romance unlike almost any other way. These moments can last for the duration of one dance or for the rest of your life. And some of these moments can be ones to remember.

CHAPTER 14

We Will Have These Moments To Remember

"To watch us dance is to hear our hearts speak."
—Hopi Indian Saying

WHEN THE FOUR Lads recorded their blockbuster hit *Moments to Remember* in the '50s, they may very well have been singing about those rare unforgettable moments a couple can live through dancing. A true Man of Confi-Dance will have moments in his life that will be highlights for both himself and the lady he is with, making these moments to remember. Some that I remember and savor, in no particular order, are as follows.

One such night was when I was in Vail Village in Colorado during a ski trip. I was the leader for this trip sponsored by the Tampa Bay Ski Club and had the good fortune to have in our group a lady from the Midwest whom I had met on a recent cruise where I was a dance host. We had lightly flirted a bit during the cruise and stayed in contact by e-mail and phone after the cruise, and when I told her about this ski trip, she decided to join the group as she loved to ski. She did have one caveat: I had to agree that we would find a time and place to get in some ballroom dancing, not an easy order to fill in Vail, Colorado, in the middle of ski season.

MOC leading dance class on slopes

Well here are some things that need to be considered when one is seeking ballroom dancing in the mountains of Colorado during ski season. First, the elevation in Vail, Colorado, is about eight thousand feet, and with this high altitude and thinner air it does not take much physical activity to get you breathing hard and gasping for air. (I try to tell the ladies that it's not about them, it's the high altitude!) Second, finding music to which one could dance any of the ballroom dances in the bars and nightspots up there is like looking for a misplaced snowball on the side of the ski slope. Third, there is hardly any live music anyway except for the weekends. And fourth, one rarely packs his dance shoes for a ski trip.

However, we went walking in beautiful Vail Village looking for some bar or venue where we could dance, with the lights twinkling in the trees, the storefronts bright and awash with fancy ski wear, expensive jewelry and fur coats, art galleries, and very upscale restaurants. As we rounded one corner in the outer edge of the Village closer to the lifts, music was playing from a speaker near a small gift shop. I recognized the song as an excellent foxtrot by Frank Sinatra and immediately stopped, took my friend's packages and laid them on the bench nearby, took her gloved hand in my gloved hand and invited her into dance position. As we did our foxtrot under lightly falling snow, our breath creating little white clouds, our noses and cheeks turning pink in the cool night air, our après-ski boots scuffing up the newly accumulated snow on the main walking area between the shops on either side, she smiled up at me in a way that makes it so right. Several people walking around paused to watch us, and when the song ended and I bowed slightly to her as I released her from dance position, a little girl, perhaps four or five years old, her cheeks rosy red from the cold, walked up to us shyly and held out a dollar bill for us! We laughed, but I also accepted the dollar of course—didn't want to hurt the little girl's feeling, right? I've hardly seen my dance partner since that ski week, but I'll bet she still remembers that moment. Obviously, I still do.

To emphasize our love of dance and the ends to which dancers will go, she and I continued walking until we found the bar two doors down that supposedly played some dance music, only to find that their band wouldn't begin until after 10:00 p.m. (much too late for us guys who have skied hard all day in the cold), but he was nice enough to let us plug in the little boom box we had with us, put in our dance CDs, and with the purchase of a beer each (no problem here), we could have their decent dance floor for about forty-five minutes. Let me tell you, trying to dance at that altitude for forty-five minutes with a lady who wants to get in as much dancing as she can when she has a partner who can dance is like a minimarathon run. We were both gasping for air frequently, both soaking wet under our sweaters, and both tired but satisfied that we got in some decent dancing on our ski trip. In fact, at the final banquet night for our ski group, the two of us did a miniexhibition of various ballroom dances (each dance about forty-five-to-sixty-second excerpts) on the carpet floor in our regular shoes.

Last year, I visited New York City with Nancy. Because she knows NYC from years of buying trips for her former ladies' boutique, she was able to make me feel comfortable in this big scary city. While there, we met up with another couple we had previously met for brunch at a restaurant that had a jazz duo playing some nice music. Here it is, almost noon on a Sunday morning in NYC, raining lightly outside, two couples enjoying a reunion in a nice restaurant just off Broadway before attending a play, and Nancy turned to me and innocently wondered out loud, "Isn't that a foxtrot they're playing?"

If the *William Tell Overture* had been playing in the background at that moment, you can bet the Lone Ranger, mask and all, would have ridden in with his dance shoes on to save the day, but instead it's now time for the Man of Confi-Dance that I am to spring into action.

"Yes, it is," I replied and smiled back. "Would you like to dance?"

Her smile, as she rose from the table to take my hand, was the only answer a Man of Confi-Dance needs, so we walked over to where the duo is playing and began a contained foxtrot in and among the several vacant tables nearby. The eyes of those sitting at other tables watching us trip the light fantastic in the middle of brunch in this upbeat restaurant in NYC is what makes us relish this moment and adds yet another memory to our collection.

Impromptu dancing on the shoreline of an ocean or a lake, in the lounge of a crowded bar, on the deck of an excursion boat in the Caribbean to steel band music, or on the sidewalk or in a park of a sleepy village on vacation are wonderful, spontaneous, and exciting moments. A Man of Confi-Dance can create these memories with ladies that will find this unexpected opportunity sheer joy and a highlight of that day, or night, or her entire vacation.

Remember the tango scene with Al Pacino in *Scent of a Woman*? It can be your scene too when you are a Man of Confi-Dance and to think he was blind! I was attending a weekend of ballroom dancing at the Neville Hotel in the Catskill Mountains of New York, just prior to boarding a ship in NYC for a cruise to New England and Canada as a dance host. I was chatting with several guys when a lady walked into the room, dressed impeccably, and with such a stunning look about her that I couldn't take my eyes off her, watching her make her way through the tables and out onto the dance floor. Without hesitation, I jumped up and made my way out onto the dance floor in pursuit of her only to watch as another guy asked her to dance before I could get close enough. I do not recall doing that before—spontaneously following a woman I'd never seen before in hopes of a dance. Maybe it was a moment like in "South Pacific" when the Frenchman sings "Some enchanted evening, you will see a stranger . . . across a crowded room . . ."

I waited for that dance to end while chatting with another dancer, Joan Miller, whom I had known from prior dance cruises where I had hosted. And when the dance ended, this dream lady came right up to Joan whom I'm still talking to—seems they were rooming together! Needless to say I was out on the floor with her the very next dance and managed to monopolize a major part of her time for the two days I was there. It was truly something that would never have happened if I were not confident enough in my ability to ask almost any lady to dance almost any dance in almost any venue where dancing is either going on or could be going on.

A few years ago, I had arranged a time share swap during the summer at a resort condo up near Coeur D'Alene, Idaho. My oldest son, Keith, agreed to be my travel mate. That is one beautiful area of the country, and we did a good bit of touring, a good bit of eating, a good bit of beer drinking, plus all of the other things you do on vacation. We decided to take a two-day jaunt into British Columbia, Canada, touching a piece of Washington, Idaho, and Montana along the way. We got as far as Nelson, British Columbia, (ever heard of it?) where we decided to stay over for the night. After wandering around the town, sampling the local Kokanee Beer (whose brewery we visited the following day on our way home), and looking for a restaurant for dinner, I spotted a small hand-written sign in the window of a small hotel lobby announcing, "Salsa lessons tonight at 7:00 p.m. in the bar."

"Salsa lessons all the way up here in Nelson, British Columbia?" I asked out loud, incredulous. But Keith and I showed up at 7:00 p.m. (he's a good son and will patronize his dad if his dad is buying the beer) to find about a dozen women ranging in age from maybe twenty to maybe sixty, about three other guys, and an excited and ready-to-go young female instructor cranking up the music. We danced for two hours. I knew basically everything she taught in the salsa and merengue and had the ladies lining up to rotate in with me nonstop. Even Keith, who doesn't do much ballroom dancing, had his hands full. It was an unexpectedly fun night and showed me that wherever you are in the world, there might just be a place that a Man of Confi-Dance will be highly in demand

My friend and fellow dance host, Howard Smallowitz, from Austin, Texas, was telling me how much he loves what being a Man of Confi-Dance has done for him. In Beijing, China, he was salsa dancing to a Colombian band with an American lady, and as he thanked her for the dance and she was walking away, she turned back and told him, "You're going to make a lot of women here happy tonight." That's what it's all about.

Howard is fifty-one and has two jobs: as a dance instructor and as a systems engineer at IBM—and likes both jobs. He's been a dance instructor for thirteen years. He never walked onto a dance floor until he was thirty-seven but got into it quickly and seriously. He started out with a salsa lesson, stayed on, and before long was teaching. I asked Howard how he saw himself as a Man of Confi-Dance.

"It used to be with my travels in my IBM job on the road, I'd go back to my hotel room and watch TV," he explained. "Now, I find where there is dancing in the town I'm in, I walk onto the floor, and within several dances, I'm everyone's best friend because of my ability to dance—at least with ladies for sure."

His next comments will probably trigger memories for most guys. "I used to stand around the walls in a bar holding an expensive beer, desperately trying to figure out how to talk to that good-looking woman over there," he remembers. Howard tells me that now he has zero problems walking up to her and asking her to dance. He then has her full attention for three-and-a-half minutes and has established an acceptable invitation to talk to her and get to know her. He says, "This is how being a Man of Confi-Dance has opened doors for me."

As a dance host, he doesn't really like cruising that much (would like more time in each port) but says, "How can you beat it when you only have to dance with ladies to see the world? It's really a high point in your life when on a cruise you have become a celebrity in a matter of days, getting compliments."

"So what was a low point in your life related to dancing?" I asked Howard.

He replied, "I remember when I was in college. It was Halloween, and I dressed as a nerd, really dorky. I had a girl friend at the time and she commented, 'Cool, you even dance like a nerd.' I still remember that comment."

That's something Howard Smallowitz, a Man of Confi-Dance, doesn't need to worry about anymore.

CHAPTER 15

The Viewpoint If You're From Venus

"I do everything the man does, only backwards
and in high heels."
—Ginger Rogers

I F LADIES DIDN'T like dancing so much, there wouldn't be much dancing for men, would there? But ladies by and large love to dance. When girls are very young, their first view of dancing may come from Cinderella at the ball or Beauty dancing with the Beast. That's very romantic and very sweet. Also parents enroll their daughters in dance schools for ballet, tap, jazz, etc., while the young boys are watching football and baseball with their dads and getting into T-ball leagues and gymnastics or swim classes at the *Y*, or similar activities. And when your fourth or fifth-grade teacher takes the whole class into the school gymnasium or cafeteria during recess on a rainy day and announces that you will all do some dancing today, the girls squeal and smile, but the boys, stomachs churning with raw fear, are ready to head for the hills.

Females of almost any age have always been ready to participate in dancing with the males in our society, but the opposite hasn't always been true. Is it because the men are expected to lead? Is it because men are naturally shyer? Is it because men do not mature as quickly as women? Is it a sign of weakness or resignation created by peer pressure among males that keeps men from participating willingly and happily?

I am not a student of psychology nor have I studied childhood development. I do not know the clinical or medical terms that would be used to describe the natural phenomena that occur when men are placed in a position of either having to or being expected to ask someone of the opposite sex to dance: heart palpitations, profuse sweating, weakness in the knees and legs, and even perhaps fear of death. That may be exaggerated a bit, but you know what I'm talking about.

If a lady wants a man to eventually sometime, someday, or somewhere dance with her, it helps to understand him and to help him finally see that he might even find this excruciating, humiliating, embarrassing, and please-don't-make-me-do-this activity fun. He might even like it! He might even want to do it again! He might even find that other men, guys who were once his allies in fighting off and hiding from ladies who wanted to be danced with, might in fact admire him and secretly wish they could do what he is doing: being the man who can dance with a lady successfully and who can create a dance moment where both partners find it enjoyable and maybe even romantic. In other words, he might actually enjoy becoming a Man of Confi-Dance.

Remember, it doesn't happen overnight. But if young girls in grade school help shy boys in a dance venue overcome their shyness or their hesitancy to even try, it will help. If girls in their teens show appreciation when a teenage boy makes the effort to dance with them at a dance or a party, it will help. If women at dances, at bars, at lounges, at social affairs that include dancing will help a man feel comfortable dancing with them by being patient and complimenting his effort, it will help. And when girls and ladies help boys and men gain their confidence on the dance floor and make them more at ease, they are helping not only their prospective partners, but they are surely helping themselves.

Let us assume that you are a lady who's been going with, or married to, a man for a number of years, and dancing is just not his thing, but you'd like it to be. You yearn for the romantic feeling that dancing gave you years before, perhaps at junior or senior high school dances, or in bars and lounges before the current man in your life came along. Yes, you wanted the man in your life to be a dancer, but you didn't make it a deal-breaker when you fell for him and decided that all of the other wonderful things that he brought into your life far overshadowed his inability and/or his unwillingness to dance with you. In so many ways, this man of yours is perfect, he's handsome, he's charming, and he's cool. You love being with him, and of course, being seen with him. So why can't he be a dancer too?

My mother told me that when she was a teenager, she dreamed of the man she would marry: He would be tall, dark, and handsome, and be a good dancer. When she met my father in 1938, it was love at first sight, and he proposed to her within two weeks of their first setting eyes on each other. He wasn't tall, he wasn't that dark, though she did think him handsome, and she knew nothing about his interest in, nor his ability to dance. But she did know she wanted to spend the rest of her life with him.

She was in for a pleasant surprise when she found out later that he could indeed dance. And they always danced whenever and wherever they went where dancing was available.

She told me stories of how my dad would be kind enough to dance with some of the other ladies in their social circles whose husbands didn't dance and how these ladies would thank her for sharing him and compliment his dancing to her. She felt like the lucky one because her man could and would dance with her. In his element, my father was indeed a Man-Of-Confi-Dance. My father passed away just about the time I was beginning to take ballroom dance lessons, and I still regret that he never taught me or influenced me regarding ballroom dancing. So when I first began competing in USABDA competitions, I used to wear his old tuxedo that still fit me perfectly so that he was there with me dancing and competing and giving me support.

We have a comic strip in our local paper called, *Rhymes with Orange*, which seems to feature what they label "The Criteria." One that I saw very recently showed two elderly ladies walking side by side, and the one with the cane in her hand was saying to the other, "I think I like him, he's a gentleman, he makes me laugh, and he can drive at night." Personally, I think they left out something more important. The other lady should have replied, "Yes, but can he dance?"

So what can a lady do if her husband or significant other won't dance with her? It certainly shouldn't be a reason to give up on him or a reason to make life unpleasant for him if he won't change his ways. But what if he learned that by making his wife or significant other happy on the dance floor, he will undoubtedly make his life more pleasant too? Is this guaranteed? No. Is it probable? Yes. That should be good enough odds guys to think about this seriously.

I saw a billboard a few months ago in Tampa, Florida, on a street that weaved through some trendy neighborhoods, that was an advertisement for a local Arthur Murray Dance Studio. Its message: "Do It For Her. Learn To Dance." Think about it, men. It's a strong message. But then a month or so later, I saw that other Arthur Murray Dance Studio billboard near Orlando, Florida, that I mentioned earlier, with an even stronger message: "Do It For Her. The Rewards Are Endless." It is a message that I personally know to be the absolute truth.

Many a lady could think back over the years she's been with her man how many times, how many places, how many evenings, and count how many opportunities she would have enjoyed getting up with him and walking out onto the dance floor, to be held in his arms, and to dance to a beautiful, sentimental, or romantic song, but it didn't happen. Her man may be romantic, he may have recognized the song playing as a special song from their past, he may enjoy humming along with it, he may smile at her, and may even hug her as she reminds him of some special and happy moments from their past, but if that's still not enough to get him to ask her to dance to it, then they are both missing out on some of the finest and sweetest moments life has to offer. The romance in their lives could be given such a boost by just an innocent little dance.

I read a quote recently in an edition of *Reader's Digest* by former football coach, Jimmy Johnson (though in a subsequent issue, someone said this quote was from Goethe): "Treat a person as he is, and he will remain as he is. Treat him as he could be, and he will become what he should be." That man of yours could become what you'd like him to be if you go about it in the right way. The rewards are very well worthwhile.

CHAPTER 16

The Viewpoint If You're From Mars

**"God respects you when you work,
but he loves you when you dance."**

—Sufi Saying

SO FOR THE man who doesn't dance, the question is why? Ladies from Venus and men from Mars will always be wondering how to understand how the other thinks. So, ladies, let's see some reasons your Martian won't dance. Maybe it's one or more of the following: He is afraid of embarrassing himself in front of others. He never learned to dance and thinks he is too cool to get up and try something for the first time in front of others. He believes he doesn't have rhythm or coordination. He thinks guys that dance are sissies or henpecked. He had some very uncomfortable episodes of dancing earlier in life and is afraid to revisit dancing now. He has always been an outsider when it comes to dancing and is not confident or comfortable enough with himself to try to become an insider. He has religious beliefs that do not allow dancing (and that should be respected). He has physical limitations to dancing in general (and this should be respected up to a point). He just doesn't seem to have a romantic streak in him. He has some underlying issues with this relationship that keeps him from wanting or enjoying anything remotely intimate. He enjoys having a root canal more than having to dance. And there must be numerous other reasons that you could add to this list.

Take heart! Most of these reasons can be overcome. But a lady must be careful, patient, wise, complimentary, helpful, and ready to start at the beginning with dance lessons with her nondancing man. Know also, ladies, that with these first lessons, his pride may be on the line too. When the instructor tells him that in most of the dances he will be learning, the man will begin with his left foot, and your man then takes his first step on his right foot, do not make fun of him or tease him. Instead, a little quiet suggestion such as "Dear, try with your *other* left foot" might break the tension and help him realize that you are in it with him.

You can take private lessons (only you two and your instructor—no others watching and often not a bad way to start out) or group lessons (much cheaper than private lessons, probably the same caliber instructor but without the personal attention, plenty of others in the class, but many in the same boat). A lady must find the right way to ask her man to take dance lessons with her (regardless of her level of dancing ability). When I started taking ballroom dance lessons, you may recall it was at the suggestion from my neighbor that dancing might lead to more romance. That was enough for me to hear. Will it be for your man? Do you want to imply or promise that? Or is there another trigger or heartstring you can rely on to coax him into this?

If this is his first exposure to ballroom dancing, or if it's been many years and he hasn't shown interest during this time, it may be tough. But somehow, some way, you should try to show him the benefits of learning to dance with you. Discuss how much it would mean to you. Show him how much happiness it would give you to have him get up and dance with you sometime somewhere in public when other people are doing the same. Let him know how much happiness it might also bring to him when you are happy. And keep trying to find the trigger that appeals enough for him to agree to this new twist in his otherwise complacent and nonthreatening life up until now. But if he does begin to learn to dance, and indeed he does find that you turn into a happier camper because of this, he will find that doors and windows will open to him.

Like most guys in general, ladies, if your man from Mars will start to learn to dance and lose his inhibitions, shyness, attitude problems, and/or any or all of the other reasons that keep men from learning to dance, there hopefully will come that point, especially in a group class, where his natural competitiveness will kick in. He will not only have acquiesced to taking the lessons, but he will want to be good at it, to look better than the other guys learning for the first time. Praise him, thank him, practice with him, reward him, and help put that chip on his shoulder. This is now just the beginning of perhaps a new phase—a new interest—in his life that he may want to pursue in a more serious way. Even if the only measure of accomplishment you gain from this entire process (ordeal for him) is that your man now has enough confidence (or at least willingness) to dance with you at your daughter's (or son's) wedding, or at some other special event in your life, you have made enormous progress. Just make sure he knows how much his efforts mean to you, how much you enjoy being in his arms like other women and their partners, how long you have waited for this moment, and how your appreciation will flow over to other areas of your life together.

And guys, even though it may sound like the approach in this chapter is written for the ladies, it is indeed all about you. Should you find yourself being urged and coddled and humored into finally taking dance lessons by one or more of the suggestions above being used by your significant other, just go with the flow. She cares about you, she loves you, and she wants to bring more romance back into your lives. Give her credit for trying, hug her for it, and go the distance with her. The rewards are endless.

CHAPTER 17

Can The Planets Possibly Be Aligned?

**"Dancing with the feet is one thing,
but dancing with the heart is another."**
—Anonymous

MOST OF US men are probably considered by most of our women as somewhat obtuse. We wouldn't know what pleases her and what displeases her if asked to make a list. We need to pay more attention.

We need to know exactly what pleases her and what does not. We need to know if something as irrelevant to us as not dancing with her displeases her and is an important issue. We need to believe that we have it in us to change that if that is the case. We need to know that buying her new jewelry, taking her on vacations, helping her with the dishes all get points. But we need to know that there are other intangibles, things almost too fearful to dwell on in our minds, things like how her face lost its glow last Saturday night when you two were out with several other couples at the country club when the band started playing a nice easy romantic song, and the other couples decided to dance. And you just sat there like a lump, staring around the room at everyone enjoying themselves, thinking what a nice evening you two were having. At that moment, I suspect that she's thinking how nice it would be if this big, adorable stick-in-the-mud next to her would only ask her to dance too and how sad she was that you wouldn't.

You never do. She's hinted at it before, but you just shrugged it off. (After all, I'm the man, and if the man doesn't want to dance, then the man doesn't have to dance. Hey, who's in charge here, anyway?)

If by some strange alignment of the planets Mars and Venus one of you guys should have a change of heart, and the two of you actually take the big step and begin dance lessons, both of you should take heed of some underlying basic facts. First of all, the man is the leader, and the lady is the follower. If that is not how your marriage or relationship works at home, that's your private business. But on the dance floor, he leads and she follows. That is what a good dance partnership needs for any chance at success, so each of you must adopt the right attitude to find success.

Next, if the man is supposed to lead, and if the man is a beginner, how is this going to happen? With patience. And time. And practice—time to practice what you learn in class, between classes, or before a dance opportunity or, quite simply, you lose it.

Other important basic facts that the two of you must remember are that not all of us learn at the same pace, not all of us are as graceful as the other, not all of us remember what we learned as well as the other, not all of us are as good at this as the other, and that it can be work at times to learn even the basics of dancing. Mars and Venus may be miles and miles apart, but here each partner must be patient with the other, be understanding and helpful, and not pick on each other or blame each other. That can put a severe strain on any relationship and lead to one or the other, or both, of you throwing in the towel. Avoid this at all cost if possible. Hopefully whatever strengths your relationship is based on will also be the strong foundation for your dancing partnership.

Both of you, man from Mars and lady from Venus, should keep the following things in mind: The man as the leader has the responsibility of hearing the beat or rhythm and knowing when to begin, and deciding what step or pattern to use, and in what order, and at the same time applying some floor craft as he navigates his way around the dance floor taking the lady with him. That amounts to multiple tasking—the various jobs he has to handle at the same time. And while he is still new at it, it can be quite overwhelming. That's when and why he needs encouragement, patience, smiles, hugs, etc., to help him through some very trying times. I've been there. I remember those days of uncertainty on the dance floor—what do I do next, how do I avoid the couple in front, or how do I get out of the way of a faster moving couple behind me?

All of the smooth dances like the tango, foxtrot, and waltz, to name the more common ones, follow a line of dance around the floor, which is circling the dance floor's perimeter in a counterclockwise direction. Slower moving couples dance closer to the center allowing the outer lanes to be used by faster and usually more-experienced dancers. Some spirited or jazzy foxtrots, for example, may sound more like a swing for some couples, while others enjoy a faster-paced foxtrot. Those couples doing the swing should move to the center of the dance floor leaving the outside lanes to those couples dancing the foxtrot allowing them to maintain the line of dance around and around the room.

I mention this because the man has to take these things into account when he is leading his partner in a dance. He will learn the proper floor etiquette as he learns more about dancing, but the responsibility of maneuvering and navigating still falls to him, and the lady must understand this and do as much as possible to make it easier for him. A beginner couple may try a pattern or step they have recently learned in a smooth dance and find themselves at the completion of their efforts facing backward to the line of dance just as other couples are coming forward into their space and thus become confused as to what to do next.

If all of this seems so daunting and overwhelming that you wonder why anyone would ever want to put themselves through all of this, just remember that anything worthwhile takes some effort to master. You may think you don't have rhythm, or you are tone deaf, or too clumsy or clunky to be a dancer, or not graceful enough to move like a dancer, but you may also be just plain wrong. Over the years in the circle of dancers in my area that have been attending the same dances I attend, I have seen unbelievable progress. I have seen couples who were taking beginner lessons and wondered *why?* I could not see them ever looking like dancers, and then one day . . . they *did!*

Another couple who began taking lessons in my town looked determined, but they also looked to me like they just would not ever amount to much on the dance floor. My thinking was, hey, if they enjoyed it, and it was a nice activity for them, so what if they never got very good. Within two years, that couple had taken more lessons than I had in ten years, practiced routinely, dropped a few pounds and firmed up, and then proceeded to beat me and my regular partner in an amateur dance competition in one of the dance categories I was sure we would win. Not only did Jeff and Sandy Kline of Lakeland earn my respect, but they taught me to never judge the level someone can attain if they work at it and want it enough. I pre-judged them, and I was just plain wrong. If you pre-judge yourselves, you also may be wrong, and that would be a shame. Go for it, if you want it, like they did. They went on to compete in many classy competitions around the country, held the top offices in our local USA Dance chapter, and are strong advocates of ballroom dancing wherever they go.

RAOUL WEINSTEIN

All of us who have danced awhile can remember when we were new at dancing and how daunting it was, and thus we try to be more understanding with beginners. Some veteran dancers however may not be as kind, so beginning dancers should not let a hostile glance or terse words aimed their way affect their attitude toward dancing—most dancers are helpful and accommodating to other dancers. We love it, and we want everyone else on the dance floor to love it as well.

Jeff and Sandy Kline in Tampa Competiton

CHAPTER 18

Be Friends On And Off The Dance Floor

**"Let us read and let us dance—two amusements that
will never do any harm to the world."**
—Voltaire

ONE OF THE areas for potential friction with a couple just beginning to learn to dance is when they practice what they've learned at home or some place without their instructor. It can be amazing how differently each one seems to remember the pattern they just learned a day or two ago. He thinks he's supposed to lead it this way, and she thinks no, it was that way! And before you know it, you are arguing over something that you may not be able to solve anyway until you consult back with your instructor at your next lesson. I've been there too with more than one dance partner.

You are better off letting your instructor be the referee than bashing each other thinking you are right and the other is wrong. It just doesn't lead to anything good. When you do get with your instructor, you would be well-advised not to argue your case; just simply ask how the step or pattern was supposed to be done. Complaints about your partner to your instructor such as "He tries to push me too far to the right when he turns me out . . ." or "She thinks I should be holding her right hand with my left hand, but I think it's my right hand . . ." may just alienate each of you, and you don't need this. A dance couple is indeed a partnership, and that means it takes both of you to be on the same sheet of music to make it happen successfully.

When Susan and I divorced, we continued to date for three more years, continued taking lessons together for much of those three years, and continued dancing at Mary's on Friday nights. We also competed a few times together during those years plus attended a dance weekend/workshop once or twice.

Then one day, Susan told me she had met a guy in a basic swing class (a class that I didn't think I needed anymore), and she was ready to move on to a life with him. They were married within the year and remain a happy couple and good friends of mine now. Without a partner, what did I do? I immediately called a lady who was part of our Friday night group at Mary's studio and asked her to go dancing with me in Tampa later that week. Barb and I began dating, became dance partners, competed, became engaged, but, alas, eventually split. But during our approximately four years together, ballroom dancing was our primary source of social life and activity. We had regularly scheduled private lessons with Mary once or twice a week, plus the group lessons, plus we danced wherever and whenever we could find places to dance.

When Barbara and I split up, I thought I would never want to dance again, at least not at Mary's Friday night group because Barbara was going to be there. But then I realized early on that I did still want to dance. I found another professional dance instructor nearby and continued my training in ballroom dancing. He was very good and had a much different style and approach than Mary, and sometimes a different way of teaching can be a good thing in helping you mold your dancing style and technique. I found it to be the best of both worlds in forging my dance repertoire.

As you learned earlier, it was then that the opportunity to be a gentleman dance host on a cruise to the Caribbean came my way, and a door was opened to unimagined travel and social experiences all because I had taken enough dance lessons and had become by that time a Man of Confi-Dance.

Over the years, these special ladies, Linda, Susan, and Barbara, who shared my life and my dance space, have remained close friends. I think the world of each of them, and I still dance with them whenever the occasion arises. While dancing was a good part of the life I had with each of these wonderful ladies, we are also still friends off the dance floor to this day. Even though romance is great and wonderful relationships that evolve can last for years, there is something very special about keeping good and caring friendships with those ladies who were your significant others in earlier years.

Section Four

ADVENTURE:
The World Can Be Yours

THERE'S NOTHING LIKE seeing the world for adventure. To see the places around the world that you've dreamed about, read about, seen on TV and in movies, and finally find yourself actually there is an unbelievable thrill and adventure. I have been so lucky to have stumbled onto a niche in 2003 that led me to being a dance host on cruise ships right up to this day all because I can dance well enough to be provided this opportunity. Well maybe a few things more as I will delve into in the following chapters.

Can a good dancer be happy, healthy, and find romance even if he is not a gentleman dance host on cruise ships? Of course. But if he can add the excitement and adventure that cruising the seven seas as a gentleman dance host can bring, I want to encourage it and be as much help as I can. So read on.

CHAPTER 19

The Art Of Being A Dance Host

"Dance first. Think later. It's the natural order."
—Samuel Beckett

A S I BECAME more experienced as a dance host on cruise ships, I began to understand my role better and better: to make each dance with each lady as nice, as comfortable, and as enjoyable an experience for her as it was possible for me to accomplish. This meant that I should be dancing with each lady at her level for the most part, concentrating on her ability to follow my lead as she picks up on the patterns I try leading her through. An experienced male dancer should be able to tell quickly and quite accurately what his partner can and can't do in the particular type of dance they are doing. The lady may well dance at a higher level of competence in smooth dances like foxtrot and waltz while not be very skilled or comfortable with some Latin dances such as rumba or cha cha.

MOC as host on Alaskan cruise

As a dance host, the many ladies I dance with have varying abilities and styles, and also varying ages, some even in their nineties! I'll say it again: It is my job when I ask a lady to dance to make this dance at this moment in time as enjoyable for her as possible. If she's very good, I will have to work hard to lead her through steps and patterns that may put me at the limits of my competence. If she's new to ballroom dancing (as all of us dance hosts were once), I must be very patient and dance simple basic patterns while giving her a good frame, a firm lead, and not get too fancy or she may become frustrated and even embarrassed. Since our cruises are usually seven to as many as sixteen days, there will be time for the new dancers to improve and for me to find the level with each of the ladies that works for us as a partnership on the dance floor. My ultimate accomplishment on a cruise is to be recognized by the ladies as a good dance host rather than a good dancer. A Man of Confi-Dance who polishes his style and techniques, and makes the enjoyment for the ladies his number one objective, will be well on his way to becoming an excellent dance host.

RAOUL WEINSTEIN

Most of my dance hosting has been on cruises originated by the company Dancers at Sea. The owner, Wendy Olsen, fifty, is from the Atlanta, Georgia, area. "I am lucky," she says, "I make a living out of my hobby, ballroom dancing."

MOC with Wendy of Dancers at Sea

Wendy, Marilyn, and Nancy all dressed up

She takes her clients and a staff of qualified and experienced dancers (many of whom are professional dancers) all around the world. Her itineraries offer some of the most exotic ports on some of the finest ships providing social dancing each day or night, setting the stage for a wonderful and memorable time. She began ballroom dancing at the age of thirty-four. Dancing is very important to Wendy since it is her livelihood, but more than that it is an immense pleasure in her life both on and off the ship.

When asked what she thought it would mean to be a Man of Confi-Dance, Wendy took her hand and pulled her chic platinum hair to one side of her forehead, paused a moment, looked me straight in the eye and replied, "He is a man who is able to enjoy himself and help his partner enjoy herself, in the moment, by embracing a variety of kinds of music while feeling attitude and playtime as a man and a woman" Whew! I like that, Wendy—I can feel it.

I asked Wendy if she did much dancing in her early years. "I always enjoyed the music of the '60s and '70s," she recalled of her youth in Utah. "At school when I was eight years old, I would organize dance time during recess instead of going out in the cold weather. I encouraged boys and girls in the lunch room to dance and avoid the blizzards outside. Later I brought my record player, and the girls and boys would line up on opposite sides of the room. It was important that we encourage the boys to have confidence to ask a girl to dance (to avoid the cold weather). As long as girls were nice to boys, there was a chance it would work—it was critical to get boys to have the courage to ask girls to dance." Sounds like a familiar story in every part of the country—one that most of us guys still remember mostly with horror!

She recalls how as she got older, she loved music, and moving her body to the rhythm—no right, no wrong, just responding to music and being uninhibited in her movements. Her church had dance lessons where she encouraged her brothers to learn and to be confident. She knew that learning to dance would be a good social discipline in their lives. (I hope they listened to her; I wish I had had an older sister tell me that when I was young!)

I met Wendy for the first time in 2004 when I was invited to do an audition cruise with her as a potential dance host. It was a five-day cruise out of Ft. Lauderdale, and I wanted to do well as Wendy had an agenda of future cruises that were much more exciting than the ones I was doing with my first company. For me, the real plum of becoming one of Wendy's regular hosts was that she had a cruise coming up on the Cunard Line's new *Queen Mary II*, and I was enticed by the thought of being on that ship and that cruise. It was a ten-day cruise to the Caribbean out of New York City.

The second night out we were dancing before dinner, an elegant time for a little dancing when everyone is rested and dressed properly for the evening. We were dancing to a trio in a circular open dance area below an atrium in the middle of the ship that probably soared seven or eight decks. I was doing a foxtrot with one of the ladies who was smiling, and glancing up noting the passengers on various floors standing by the railings looking down at us tripping the light fantastic. I could just imagine one of those ladies up above watching us elbowing her husband in the ribs and chiding him, "You see that, Herman, if you would just take some lessons with me, we could be doing that too!" These are the moments the ladies in our dance group long for and live for—being beautifully dressed up and in the arms of a Man of Confi-Dance while dancing in an elegant setting where they are seen, and probably envied, by strangers.

Dieter, Mama Lee, and RW

Dancers At Sea (DAS) group photo

Near the end of the cruise I held my breath in anticipation of Wendy's decision of my audition and was overjoyed when she said quite casually, "Consider yourself one of my dance hosts and let me know which of my upcoming cruises you'd like to join." I immediately signed on for the *Queen Mary II* cruise and have been able to pick and choose my way around the world as a dance host with Wendy and Dancers at Sea for all these years since. She has always left the door open to me and has never refused to include me as a dance host on any of her cruises that I have requested, for which I am immensely appreciative.

When I asked her recently about her first encounter with a Man of Confi-Dance, Wendy replied that she married the first real Man of Confi-Dance she met. She was newly divorced and decided on a cruise vacation. She was spending time in the disco and casino and was in her comfort zone.

Wendy reminisces, "I met a guy in the casino, we laughed, we struck up a conversation, and he wanted to introduce me to his roommate. He even pleaded. So I entered the ballroom and watched this man who would be my future husband dancing. I was introduced to him and taken into his arms for a dance—unprepared but ended up marrying him," she smiles.

How did it feel dancing with him? "One of the first compliments he paid to me when I got over my jitters," she continued, "was his assurances that he would lead me, which put me at ease, and enabled me to enjoy the dance without worry."

Is this a real Man of Confi-Dance or what? Is it always that easy to snag a life partner? One thing Wendy knows well is what it takes for a dancer to be a Man of Confi-Dance. On every one of her cruises she, and the ladies she brings aboard her cruises, observe her dance hosts as Men of Confi-Dance.

CHAPTER 20

I Can Dance—So What Else Do I Need?

"A dance is a measured pace, as a verse is a measured speech."
—Francis Bacon

CERTAINLY THE MOST basic requirement to being a gentleman dance host aboard a cruise ship and opening the door to new adventure is your dancing ability. But if you want to be invited back again and again, there are other factors to be considered, and you should give much careful thought to these in advance if you have any desire to do some dance hosting: personality, personal hygiene, physical shape, wardrobe, social skills, leisure time, finances, family status, team player, ulterior motives, ease with travel, and rule follower. We will now visit each of these. Many of these are of value regardless of whether you host or simply want to be aware of how to treat a lady. You have the edge in her little black book if your mark is an A for etiquette.

Personality

We're talking about *your* personality here of course, and whether you are the type that would fit in with a group of ladies and fellow dance hosts in a sometimes confining and close atmosphere. Dance hosts, at least with the groups that I go to sea with, are expected to sit with the group for dinner and to rotate from table to table each night, socializing with the ladies in conversation, some light humor, and camaraderie. This is almost always an enjoyable part of the job, but if you sit at the table like a dead fish or with a bored expression on your face, find another hobby. I enjoy meeting new people and making friends. I also love telling jokes, and it is hard not to do so with new acquaintances (hey, a new audience for my old worn-out jokes!) Conversation will often trigger jokes as well as those being told by others at the table. It is very important not to lead this seemingly innocent way of keeping the conversation lively and humorous into a level of impropriety that would offend some of the ladies at your table—leave that up to the ladies! If they want to take their jokes to a new level, they can get by with it.

Personal Hygiene

The last thing the ladies want, and that includes your fellow dance hosts too is someone in their midst who smells of body odor or hasn't brushed their teeth. Dancing is a close encounter activity and oral hygiene and deodorant along with clean fresh clothes is a must for a dance host. We dance hosts often perspire more than anyone else, and it is not uncommon for a dance host to go through one or more changes of clothes during an evening of dancing. Groups that specialize in cruises for ballroom dancers usually provide one dance host for every three ladies in the group and sometimes even a smaller ratio. Thus, we dance hosts are dancing every dance while rotating our way through the ladies in our group. It can be nonstop dancing for hours some nights. I will tell you that it can be work, but its enjoyable work—I wouldn't be doing it if I didn't enjoy it. But poor personal hygiene will not help the others around you enjoy it very much and might lead some to vote for your being keelhauled!

Physical Shape

As you can tell from the preceding paragraph, we do some serious dancing each evening, and a host has got to be in good shape. These ladies have paid a premium to be on a cruise and in a group where dance hosts are provided for them. And by gosh, they want to be danced with, and we're the guys brought aboard to do that dancing, and if we have to stop and rest too often or can't catch our breath or start limping after an hour or pull a groin muscle the second night out, these ladies will not be happy. I've marveled more than once at the perseverance and stamina of some of the ladies (some older than I am) who won't quit until the bands stop playing for the night. They don't usually have regular dance partners at home, and this is their time to capitalize on all of the dancing they can. So be willing, but also be able, to do what it takes to keep these ladies dancing for the required time each day and night. (See Appendix B for more information on the multitude of health benefits derived from dancing.)

Wardrobe

Dance hosts must be able to dress the part. Each cruise will have at least two formal nights, and longer cruises will normally have more. I was once on an eleven-day Mediterranean cruise on the Cunard Lines, and they had five formal nights. That is really pushing it, but they do like to dress up for their galas: Formal Night, Black-and-White Ball, Venetian Ball, Ascot Ball, Masquerade Ball, and maybe Victorian Night.

We were in Lisbon, Portugal, and after returning to the ship after a wonderful tour of the countryside and a neat old town in the hills, I decided to sit and read out by the pool as the late afternoon was still glorious. I nodded off and lay there a little too long getting a little more sun than I needed. That night was the Ascot Ball, and dressed in my tuxedo, I joined our group for a little dancing before dinner. When one of the ladies jokingly asked me why I wasn't wearing an ascot, I smiled, pointed to my reddened face, and replied without any hesitation, "Unfortunately my 'ascot' burned today!"

These formal nights are the nights the ladies are in their prime on these cruises. If they have to pay for an extra suitcase or two on their flights there and back, they don't care! They will bring a fancy dress to wear each night, each with its own accessories—they spend months preparing for this—with careful planning for each formal night and for each of the other nights too. And they are expecting us guys to also look the part, which means we dress formally on those nights too and not the same tuxedo outfit each time. Plus we dress in sporty dance shirts and slacks on regular nights or coats and ties on dressy but not formal events. Over the years that I have been dance hosting, I have accumulated quite an array of dance shirts and try to keep pace with the ladies as best as I can. Now that the airlines are charging more for luggage, it's getting tougher to bring as much wardrobe and not pay through the nose. They do have laundries aboard most cruise ships (you can meet the nicest ladies who want to be so helpful to a helpless man attempting to wash, dry, and fold his laundry) that you can use yourself, so that helps.

Having the right luggage can be a huge factor, as is knowing how to pack. Throwing all your stuff into big bags and getting to the ship with a bag full of wrinkled clothes would be senseless. Bringing too much or bringing too little can create headaches for you as well. I have prepared a packing list on my computer (so I can update it as needed), and I print out a copy and use it for guidance before each cruise. This list doesn't count out how many of each item to pack, but reminds me not to forget basic essentials. Packing a tuxedo and forgetting the cummerbund and tie set or cufflinks and studs for the shirt can be a disaster, as can bringing your dress shoes and walking shoes and not packing your dance shoes. I must also take into account the climate and weather conditions in the area where we will be cruising and have the right clothes along. I have shivered in cold weather ports before by not being prepared and have perspired in sultry weather ports by wearing too much. But that just takes a little bit of time on the internet to properly prepare.

Regarding luggage, consider how you will handle those bags you are taking whether you will check them all or have some carry-ons, and how you will manage when you get to your final destination and find yourself schlepping more bags than you can handle through customs and the airport. Sometimes it just takes a few trips to figure out what works best for you.

Social Skills

As well as having a pleasant and even-tempered personality, having adequate social skills can play an important role too for the dance host. Proper manners at the dinner table each night are much appreciated by the others as well as generally helping the evening go by pleasurably for the people in the group, men, and ladies alike. But don't get too social with one of the ladies at your table by monopolizing her in one-on-one conversation too much or it will get back to the person in charge of your group—the person who decides whether to bring you back again (or not) as a dance host. If you and one of the ladies find a mutual attraction, so be it, but wait until after the cruise to do something about it. Go too far and you may find yourself put off the ship at the next port and having to get home on your own.

Leisure Time

To be a dance host, you must be in a position to be away from your job, your business, or whatever you do. Many hosts, like myself, are retired and have found dance hosting to be a wonderful way to see the world, meet many fine new friends, practice and improve your dance skills, and basically enjoy some of the good things in life. If you can't find the time to do this properly, wait to become a dance host when you can.

Finances

While your cruise is typically paid for by the companies you go out with (some dance hosts are placed on ships by agents who charge the hosts a daily commission, usually around $30/day), or the cruise lines themselves, there are still many expenses you will incur as a dance host. Travel to and from the port is not always covered by the company—some do and some don't for me. I have used my frequent flier points to help with a number of international flights. There will be incidentals aboard the ship such as alcoholic beverages and the gratuities that are tacked onto your shipboard bill. Some companies help with these expenses and some do not. You might need some dry cleaning on board, and of course money to take shore excursions provided by the ship, or to go touring on your own in the various ports of call. One of my biggest pleasures is to have a good cold local beer when ashore in each port. Some of them, depending on the currency exchange rates, have not been cheap like that Tuborg draught at an outside plaza in Copenhagen, Denmark, that converted back to about US$12; but hey, if you're going to be a world traveler, you have to pay the price. I made up for that expensive beer when we docked at Margarita Island off the coast of Venezuela on a Holland America cruise aboard the *Volendam*. I could buy two local beers for under a dollar! Don't forget to factor in how many dollars you may not be making while you are away from your job or business. Finally, keep in mind the souvenirs you will certainly purchase to bring home for yourself and presents for family and friends.

Family Status

Most dance hosts are single. Married guys aren't going to be getting away to go dance with other ladies that easily nor guys in a committed relationship. Familial responsibilities have to be considered. Maybe the group that wants you as a dance host would allow your wife or significant other to pay their way as one of the ladies in the group so you both get a nice vacation, albeit a working vacation for you as a host. I've done that several times with Nancy, and it has worked well for us. It has allowed us to see a part of the world we'd like to see together, and she's happy sharing dancing with me at the same ratio that I dance with the other ladies in the group. She also gets plenty of quality dancing with the other hosts as well.

Team Player

A dance host is part of a team with the other dance hosts in the group. It's important that we respect each other on and off the dance floor when we are in contact with the ladies. On the floor, we must watch how we are positioned and moving about the dance floor so as to allow our fellow hosts room to dance properly with their partners. This also goes for any other dancers on the floor. Some dancers will naturally follow the line of dance when appropriate while other less experienced dancers may not be aware of this floor etiquette. Our team of dance hosts is expected to also rotate evenly and equitably through the ladies in our group—being careful not to ask the best dancers or the best looking dancers more than their fair share. Of course, as the cruise goes on, we each begin to know the capabilities, or lack thereof, of the individual ladies in the various dances that will be played during the evening and try to take this into consideration when possible. If I ask an older, somewhat fragile lady for the next dance because I believe she is up next for me, and then the band starts up with an arduous dance like a fast hustle or samba, I might have to revert to something a little tamer with this particular lady for this particular dance. If I hear the number the band is beginning before I have invited a lady to dance, I may shift my thinking and select a different lady, one who can comfortably handle and enjoy this dance. The ladies know when we hosts get out of balance, and if some ladies are being asked to dance too often or some not enough, they will make comments to the people in charge of our group, and we hosts will hear about it later. A lady who sits out four or five dances in a row gets a bit frustrated and may not recall that twenty minutes ago she danced three or four times in a row. Overall, if the ratio for this group on this cruise is one host for three ladies, then she should average one out of every three dances. But it doesn't work out that obviously; nevertheless, by the end of the evening if she has danced about one third of the dances, regardless of the order in which this was accomplished, then we have done our jobs properly.

MOC leading NC2S workshop on cruise

MOC leading workshop with Wendy on cruise

Ulterior Motives

What could sound more romantic than to be surrounded by a group of lovely ladies each wanting you to dance with them and to hold them in your arms while you cruise across the high seas into and out of exotic ports of call, dining on fine foods in elegant dining rooms, enjoying dressy formal nights and the captain's cocktail parties, while forgetting completely who you really are when you are home? The Man of Confi-Dance dance host will not take long to realize this is a recipe for romance if he wants to let it happen. It is easy to let it happen, but if you want to remain a dance host, this is taboo. No ulterior motives allowed here. If this is what you want, do not become dance hosts, or do it but don't expect to do it for very long. Dance hosts who go beyond the proper and accepted behavior have been known to be put off the ship at the next port by those that employed them to find their own way home at their own expense. It isn't always easy not to be swayed or enticed by one or more of the ladies on a cruise. While romance is not supposed to be on a host's list of allowed activities aboard ship as a dance host, that doesn't mean that the ladies have to abide by the same rules. They often have their own agendas, and a Man of Confi-Dance might often find himself the object of affection or desire by one or more of the ladies he's dancing with. So what's a poor guy to do?

RW celebrating New Year's Eve on cruise

MOC hosting on New Year's Eve cruise

CHAPTER 21

Let's Take A Break And Visit The Confessional Booth

"I do not try to dance better than anyone else.
I only try to dance better than myself."
—Mikhail Baryshnikov

TIME FOR A confessional, I guess. On the very first cruise I took as a dance host aboard the Norwegian Sun, I found myself attracted very much to one of the ladies. There were thirty-five ladies in our group, and twelve of us dance hosts. But it didn't take long for my eyes to sort through the ladies and land on this particular one. Being aware of the rules of engagement for dance hosts, I did nothing improper, but after the third day, it became apparent that she was attracted to me as I was attracted to her. This attraction became stronger as the seven-day cruise went on, but we did nothing about it. She had a significant other at home, someone who didn't dance (sucker!), and thus she was not in a position to become involved. And that's how we left it.

But after being so low for months over my recent breakup, just the experience of being attracted to a lady and in return having her being attracted to me was powerful therapy. I came home feeling so much better about myself because of what happened (and what didn't happen). We stayed in touch via e-mail for a little while, and then she came on another cruise aboard the Norwegian Star where I was a dance host, and the same thing happened again. We shared a mutual attraction that seemed to have grown stronger but since nothing had changed on the home front in her life, nothing therefore changed with us. We felt it, we enjoyed the feelings, and once again that's how we left it.

About a year and a half later on a one-week cruise to Alaska aboard Holland America's *Oosterdam*, our group of dancers was wrapping up the second night of dancing up top in a lounge overlooking the water and the lights from ashore from both the port and starboard sides. They were playing a waltz for the final dance at midnight, and we were down to three dance hosts and only two ladies left. The other two hosts were quicker than I was, whisking the two ladies onto the dance floor. Watching them dance, I became aware of a very well-dressed attractive lady across the dance floor trying to get my attention. And yes, she was a blonde. When I looked back her way, she motioned to have me dance with her. We dance hosts are not allowed to dance with ladies who are not part of our group—the protocol is that they have not paid the premium to the company sponsoring the dance hosts, and are therefore not entitled to our "services." But it was the last dance, I didn't want to hurt her feelings by shaking my head from across the room without an explanation, plus the lady in charge of our group had already turned in for the night, so what the heck. I smiled, got up, and walked out onto the dance floor to meet her from her side, and we danced the waltz. Did I mention that she was blonde and quite attractive?

She was reasonably good and said she had been watching all of us ballroom dancers, loved to dance, had been taking ballroom dance lessons for about two years, and wished she could be dancing the night away like we were. After the dance, we each walked back to our respective tables, I was ready to turn in myself when my dance host roommate, Ben Edeling, suggested we go over and socialize for a few minutes with the couple who was sitting with the lady who had just danced with me since the couple beside her was part of our group. So we chatted with them for almost an hour, allowing me to talk to and get to know Nancy a bit. She was there with her parents who were celebrating their sixty-fifth wedding anniversary, and she envied seeing us in action on the dance floor the first night. She learned about our group sponsor, how we operated, and was disappointed that we could not dance with her in the evenings. I also found myself giving her the once-over, thinking that she looked and sounded very good, but of course, I knew that nothing should or could become of this innocent meeting on my part. But that's not what she thought, I learned later!

Ben and I walked her back to her stateroom on the way to ours, but the next day at sea, during a break in our afternoon dance lesson, I was looking for the restroom outside of the lounge we were using, when who should be walking down the stairwell adjacent to me but Nancy. I hurriedly told her I enjoyed meeting her last night, and perhaps we could meet for a drink in one of the bars at midnight when I got off work. We did, and thus began a beautiful shipboard romance that was completely unintended. I conducted myself in a way I thought was in keeping with my responsibilities and standards as a dance host with the group I was with. I did not shirk my duties or my times of being with our group for dinner, for dancing in the evenings, for lessons on days at sea, etc. Nancy and I would get together after midnight or during the days ashore, but alas, some of the ladies in our group saw us ashore in one port walking along holding hands, and I guess it just doesn't go over well with them. Maybe they were just trying to be protective of their dance host!

The bottom line was as follows: The lady who owned the company, Elly Engberg of Let's Dance Cruises, that brought me on board as a dance host never mentioned this after-hours romance once to me during the cruise, thanked me for a good job when we finished, and then never called me to be a dance host with her again. Nancy and I went on to see each other several times over several months, but we lived several states apart, and I had other considerations as well in my life at this time. I made a decision to end the budding relationship I had with Nancy.

The saga continues. After almost two and a half years of what seemed at first a good relationship with a lady in Lakeland, we recognized it was not working out as hoped and decided to end our relationship. I was leaving soon for Tahiti to be a dance host with Dancers at Sea aboard the *Tahitian Princess*, so the trip was a distraction for my sad feelings, and I looked forward, ready to move on. I just didn't know I would be moving on in such an unexpected way halfway around the world.

I was standing in a long line at night in the customs area of the airport in Tahiti after a tiring day of flying from Florida to California followed by the long nonstop flight from Los Angeles to Tahiti. You actually go across the time line and get there two days later! As the line snaked back on itself, I looked over at another part of the line, and there was Nancy! I was stunned. I was also prepared to have her walk up to me and slap me right across the face. We had had no contact during the past two and a half years when I had abruptly ended our budding relationship with a sudden phone call. She smiled though, and we greeted each other, I very warily. She was a late addition to the dance group I was hosting with. I had no idea she was coming on this cruise. She had found out via an e-mail that I was listed as one of the dance hosts, causing her to have second thoughts. She wondered if I were married, and if so, would my wife be with me. I told her I had recently begun the parting-of-the-ways process with my current lady before embarking on this trip.

We were friendly toward each other for the first couple of days, and then I invited her to join me and two of the other dance hosts on a tour of Bora Bora, which she accepted. It made sense to me—four of us sharing the vehicle was less expensive than three of us sharing the expense, right? Well, that and the fact that she was much better looking than the other two dance hosts—at least to me, that is. The warm waters of Bora Bora can be very healing, and we reconnected that day and have settled into a comfortable and committed relationship since that cruise. Dancing is good. Life is good.

That night, I went to Wendy Olsen, the owner of Dancers at Sea, and asked her over a drink before dinner in the bar if she remembered my telling her about a shipboard romance I had had several years ago when hosting with another company. She smiled and replied jokingly, "Why, do you want to have another one?" To which I replied, "She's on this cruise. In fact she's in our group." Wendy guessed immediately who it was and has since treated us as special friends because we reconnected on her cruise. As long as I kept up my end of my dance hosts duties and didn't do something too obvious or improper, she was fine with it. Most of the others in the group never caught on, and those that did seemed happy for us. But this is more the exception than the rule as to how shipboard romances are viewed by the companies hiring you as a dance host, and it is best to not fall prey to advances or come-ons by the ladies you are to dance with while hosting no matter how tempting it can be.

Raoul dancing on cruise with Nancy

RAOUL WEINSTEIN

I talked with Elly Engberg recently—our first conversation since that cruise in Alaska years ago when I first met Nancy. I told her that I was now in a committed relationship for over three years with the lady I had met on that cruise. She told me that my shipboard romance with Nancy on her cruise had caused her to adopt a more stringent policy regarding her dance hosts and any improper liaisons with the ladies on board her cruises. I do agree with her attitude She has a business to run which requires keeping her ladies happy, and I crossed her line. For me, I'm sorry to have lost the opportunity to do more hosting with Elly. But also for me, I found a wonderful lady who is part of my life now and have no regrets. This is our happy ending that brings to mind a favorite movie that always touches me. Although this wasn't exactly Cary Grant and Deborah Kerr in *Affair to Remember*, it also wasn't that far off either.

CHAPTER 22

Whoa, You Mean There's Even More To Being A Dance Host?

**"Dancing is an art that imprints the soul.
It is with you every moment;
it expresses itself in everything you do."**
—Shirley MacLaine

S INCE I CAN'T think of anything that has been more enjoyable, brought more adventure to my life, or given me more of a sense of accomplishment because of my dance skills than being a gentleman dance host, I continue to want to make this opportunity for other men a realistic possibility and even a goal. So let's address some other aspects of what is either required or important in one becoming a dance host on cruise ships.

Hosting with Lennie Corbett of Dancing Over the 7 Seas

MOC's work is never done. With Wendy in Quebec

MOC on break between dance sets on cruise

Rule Follower

A dance host must follow those rules required by the company or group that bring him onboard to be a dance host. I've already mentioned that dance hosts should avoid liaisons with the ladies or board, and an example where I did not follow these rules to the letter. But being a rule follower also means walking the walk and dressing the dress as expected. It means being on time for dinner with the group, for dance lessons with the group on most days at sea, and especially for dancing with the group. If you want to do things your way by your rules, you will find yourself no longer in demand as a dance host with most companies.

The first time I went with Lennie Corbett's company from St. Petersburg, Florida, called Dancing Over the 7 Seas, I thought telling Lennie how I'd seen things done on other cruises where I had hosted would be appreciated. His quick response was, "I've been doing this for over ten years, and I know how it works for me and my ladies. It's a business, and this is how we will do it."

He was absolutely right. I needed to follow his rules, not tell him how somebody else did things. Like a good football team, there is only one person calling the plays—leave that job to that one person. I've hosted with Lennie several times, and his system seems to work just fine—the ladies like it, Lennie keeps them happy, and I adapted to his ways in no time.

Ease With Travel

This topic might sound obvious but consider the different elements of travel that you must contend with being a cruise ship gentleman dance host. Are you prone to sea sickness? The seas can get rough no matter where you sail and no matter how big the ship. Yes, they have stabilizers and are being designed better and better, but there can be, in the words of Jerry Lee Lewis, "a whole lotta' shakin' goin' on" out there. I think the roughest I've experienced while hosting was on the traverse from New Zealand to Tasmania off the Australian coast. It's about a thousand miles of open water on the Tasman Sea, and the wind just tears at you from out of the west as we sailed right into it. The swells reached seventeen or eighteen feet, the wind was extremely strong, and our ship was really, in the words of Chuck Berry, "a reelin' and a rockin'." Bottles were falling off the shelves in the bar, souvenirs off the displays in the shops and boutiques aboard, and walking (let alone dancing) around the ship was a real challenge.

The captain decided to slow our speed down to six knots from the usual twenty-two knots, and it was still rough. For safety's sake, they called off the show in the ship's theater that involved the singers and dancers. But did our ladies take heed of any of this? Absolutely not. They had paid to be danced with each night, and by gosh they wanted us guys to dance with them as if nothing was out of the ordinary. And we did.

It takes a lot of skill to execute the various patterns in the various ballroom dances, but with the ship bucking and sliding under our feet, a whole new dimension was added. We may have looked like drunken sailors trying to navigate a tango on a roiling ship, but if that's what it took to please the ladies, we needed to be ready. It may not have been the best level of dancing we've ever exhibited on ship, but we survived. However, a lady dancing in another lounge fell and broke her wrist badly enough to require surgery in Melbourne, Australia, our next port of call, where she had to stay behind for recovery.

Loyalty

If you are as fortunate as I have been being able to be a dance host with several different companies, you must maintain the proper loyalty to that company when you are cruising with them. This may also sound obvious, but there are subtle ways you may do or say things that may have some immediate or future harm to the company you represent on this cruise.

The most important item of loyalty is not to be advertising for another company with the ladies who are with this company on this cruise. It is easy when your next job as a dance host is with another company to mention it casually at dinner or when asked when you will be cruising again. It is flattering for one or more ladies to ask when and where you will be hosting again, but divulging that information may be considered disloyal to the current company. This is a prime reason that some company owners will simply not employ dance hosts that are still being employed by other companies.

Another form of loyalty is perhaps more subtle and took me a few times to understand. When I am a dance host on a cruise, I am just another passenger as far as the ship is concerned. I am not a dance host for the ship, do not work for the ship, and have no fiduciary or representative status as far as the ship is concerned. So it seemed perfectly normal for me to voice a complaint from time to time in front of some of the ladies, either about the quality of the food at a given meal or the type of music being played by a particular band in one of the lounges. I'm a passenger like everybody else and should be entitled to my opinion, right? Wrong—if it casts a negative light on any part of this cruise, and in turn, on the company I am working for. Bottom line learned here: I am here with this company as a dance host, and I should not be saying or implying things that in any way make any aspect of this cruise less positive or less enjoyable for the participants in our group. Period.

Let me tick off a few more things that come to mind that you should take into consideration before becoming a dance host and embarking on a new world of travel and adventure:

1. Planning and securing travel to and from the ship's docks for the embarking and debarking ports.
2. Hauling and handling your luggage during your travel to and from the cruise.
3. Keeping your wardrobe as fresh and unwrinkled as possible during the cruise considering the lack of closet and dresser drawers available in the small cabins to which we dance hosts are normally assigned to share.
4. Not being overly susceptible to picking up a bug while ashore in some of the out-of-the-way ports of call, especially not drinking the local water. (I like to get my water ashore by drinking a bottle of the local beer whenever possible—strictly for health reasons, of course!)
5. Adjusting quickly and easily to the changes in time when you fly to a port many time zones different from the one you left while handling jet lag, plus the time changes that come up during the cruise. Flying from Florida to Vancouver, British Columbia, to pick up an Alaskan cruise puts you three hours off of your normal routine, and then you find yourself dancing until midnight in the new time zone almost upon arrival.

It may sound like it's impossible to be able to handle all of these considerations capably and competently, but if you can, dance hosting offers a wonderful world to dive into whenever possible. Sailing to ports and countries you've never seen before, dining on some of the finest cuisine in the world, meeting and dancing and touring with some of the nicest people you'll ever meet is just the beginning. And to think this can be yours because basically you are a Man of Confi-Dance, along with many or most of the other attributes mentioned earlier. I have worked beside fellow dance hosts as young as their midtwenties and as old as their mideighties. Many are dance instructors with superb credentials in their field, and others are just regular guys who can dance well enough to be invited by the ladies and gentlemen who run companies that specialize in cruises for ballroom dancers. In many cases they are invited directly by the cruise lines.

The Cunard Line still brings a complement of gentlemen dance hosts on each of their cruises. I have been on Cunard cruises aboard the new *Queen Mary II* and the even newer *Queen Victoria*, both ships having larger dance floors than those on most other ships. These ships are very elegant and feature a seven-piece orchestra in their ballrooms each night for dancing. Their dance hosts are always introduced to the passengers properly, and these men invite the single ladies (or ladies without partners) to dance each night whenever music and dancing is on the ballroom agenda. They love when our groups are on their cruises since our ladies are, on average, better dancers than the average single lady aboard the typical cruise. It gives them a chance to enjoy more good dances. And let's face it, dance hosts do enjoy dancing with a good partner whenever they can, as they will be dancing with many ladies who are not good dancers each evening as part of their job. That doesn't mean, as I pointed out earlier, that a dance host will dance only or more often than is appropriate with the better dancers.

I have not been a dance host with a cruise line yet, though I was invited once to do a two-week stint as a dance host on the very upscale Crystal Line several years ago. It conflicted with a New Year's cruise where I had already accepted an invitation to host. Besides, almost all of the cruise lines like their hosts to be out for three weeks or more, and that has not yet been something that's been workable for me and my lifestyle. I have not wanted to be away that long at one time. But for some of the retired guys I've met hosting with the cruise lines, it seems to fit them fine, and they seem happy with their lot. Can you blame them?

On that first cruise I took as a dance host with Let's Dance Cruises for the USABDA's first sanctioned cruise on 2003, one of the other dance hosts who was already a regular with Let's Dance Cruises was Dieter Wuennenberg, now sixty-five. Dieter already had the experience of several dance host cruises and looked like he knew the ropes. When Let's Dance Cruises invited me back to host with them again, Dieter was there, and we became good friends. In fact, he and I auditioned together for Dancers at Sea and were assigned to be roommates. I was watching him unpack his bags when he lifted at least a dozen matching cummerbund and bowtie sets in various colors of the rainbow out of his suitcase.

I said, "Dieter, this is just a five-day cruise and there is only one formal night."

He smiled mysteriously and said, "I know."

I learned on that cruise, and on several subsequent cruises with Dieter as a fellow host, that he would casually talk with the ladies at dinner and during dance time and innocently find out what color dresses they would be wearing for formal night. He would then decide which lady he wanted to impress by wearing his cummerbund and tie to match the color of her gown.

MOC with Dieter and his colorful cummerbund

Good, old, sly Dieter, the same guy that on that same auditioning cruise, and on some of the others later on, would buy and hand out a rose to each lady on formal night. On the popular TV show *The Bachelor*, a rose would be handed out to every lady but the one that was being eliminated that night. But Dieter, he never eliminated anybody—every lady was treated by his kindness, and it was one of those things about him that made him such a popular host with the ladies.

I spoke to Dieter recently and learned that since moving a few years ago from the West Palm Beach area of Florida to The Villages in central Florida, he has established himself as the local Man of Confi-Dance. Finding hardly any dancing available in the entire complex, he went to the powers that be and was told if he wanted dancing, he could do something about it. And he did.

"We let it be known that we were starting a dance club," he told me, "and within thirty hours we had sold out the maximum one hundred thirty-two spots available. This club has a dance on the first Saturday night of the month. We then had to start another club, and now another one hundred thirty-two members attend our other dance on the third Saturday night of the month."

Dieter had never been a dancer until he was forty-eight, when he broke both knees in an accident doing his job as a firefighter. Extensive rehab therapy involved doing step aerobics for over a year with another guy who had been a ballet dancer before his accident. He told Dieter he had good rhythm and wondered if he was a dancer too.

Dieter related, "He told me I should try it, and I did when I was better and began country and western dancing. After moving to South Florida and going to the Gold Coast Ballroom down there, I realized I needed to learn some ballroom dancing. I slowly shifted my style of dancing, which is different and sort of sticks out from the various ballroom dances and have been comfortable with that ever since. It may be different and not as structured, but it works for me and for the ladies I dance with."

RW and Dieter with matching dance shirts

On a typical night of hosting on a cruise, Dieter and I would sometimes coordinate the same colors in dance shirts several nights in a row to get comments from the ladies. At least once or more a night we would move close to where the other was dancing a spot dance like a rumba or cha cha or swing, make eye contact with each other and subtly nod, move ourselves and our partners so that we were facing the other couple, each with the lady on our right side, and then right on beat switch partners with each other. The ladies were taken by surprise of course, but enjoyed it, as did anyone else nearby and especially nondancers sitting in the lounges where we were dancing. I do want to caution any guy reading this not to try switching your dance partner with another guy's lady, unless he is someone you know and he knows what's going on. Especially if you're in a country and western bar!

I learned from watching Dieter hosting over the years on a number of cruises that he is certainly a Man of Confi-Dance and makes the ladies happy with his dancing. It taught me that successful dance hosts, like Men of Confi-Dance, come in many different packages, each with his own unique style and manner for making ladies happy on the dance floor. So remember, there is always room for another Man of Confi-Dance and another good dance host.

CHAPTER 23

Do I Have To Be Out On A Rocking Ship?

"We dance for laughter, we dance for tears, we dance for madness, we dance for fears, we dance for hopes, we dance for screams, we are the dancers, we create the dreams."
—Anonymous

WHILE BEING A dance host on an elegant cruise ship is certainly a first-class way to enjoy the benefits of being a Man of Confi-Dance, there are many other options. After all, being a dance host is basically being in a position at some dancing venue where you would be expected to dance with ladies who are in need of a dance partner in exchange for some form of compensation or benefit.

The regular dances put on by various USA Dance chapters are a prime venue for dance hosts. Many chapters find themselves with many more female members in regular attendance than there are available men. Notice that by using the term "available men," I am referring to men who are in a position, and also willing, to dance with the ladies in attendance that do not have dance partners. It is common for the unattached men that attend these dances to concentrate their efforts on the best female dancers or the best looking female dancers in attendance. Hey, they paid their way in; they can dance with whom they want as long as these ladies accept their invitations to dance. But what happens to those ladies who are not as much in demand?

It is usual for men invited to be dance hosts to be given free admission to the dances, and in many cases they are paid a nominal fee for acting as dance hosts. I have been invited in this capacity from time to time. It is a compliment to be considered a Man of Confi-Dance and be invited to be a dance host, and when it works into my schedule, I am happy to step up to the plate and fulfill my responsibilities to the best of my abilities.

There are many dance camps and dance weekends held all over the country where dance hosts are employed so that the ladies know they will have enough competent dance partners on hand and can count on a reasonable amount of dancing if they attend. One of my dance host friends from Long Island, Jon Forsberg, wouldn't miss the Stardust dance weekends in the Catskill Mountains of Upstate New York. He works hard and dances for many hours, but he loves to dance, especially with the many ladies he meets every time he comes to one of these weekends, and enjoys making new friends on the dance floor when he attends. And don't think for a moment that the only ladies he dances with are beginners or wallflowers or elderly ladies barely able to move around on the dance floor. He dances with some of the best dancers around, and they appreciate his abilities, his stamina, and his contagious smile reflecting the enjoyment he is feeling while dancing with each of these ladies.

Fellow dance host, Jon Forsberg

RAOUL WEINSTEIN

I have been a dance host with Jon on several cruises and roomed with him once on a cruise to Alaska. The first night, preparing for bed, Jon turned off all of the cabin lights to check out where any light might be seeping into the room. Turns out he is a light sleeper and can't stand even a hint of light when he's ready to sleep. He grabbed a bath towel from the bathroom and laid it on the floor in front of our cabin door to block the little bit of light coming in from the passageway outside. He then turned the lights out again to survey the darkness once more. The lights went on again. Jon searched his carry-on bag, found a roll of white adhesive tape, cut off a strip, and reached up and taped over the tiny red light on the smoke detector on the ceiling. Smiling, he turned off the lights again for his next inspection only to turn them on again after just a few seconds. Out came a black magic marker from his bag. He reached up and blackened the white adhesive tape that he had already applied to the smoke detector! Once more the lights out and he was satisfied. He then donned his black sleeping mask over his eyes, bid me a good night, and turned off the lights for the final time that night. The point here is to accept the idiosyncrasies of your roommates and smile. Every personality is different, and often you will remember their uniqueness longer than their jokes.

I attended one of those weekends in the Catskills as I mentioned earlier. The entrance to the dance floor in the main ballroom from the seating area was quite narrow, and the only ingress and egress to and from the floor was crowded with two-way traffic between each dance. It doesn't take long for these ladies to recognize who the male dancers are that they want to dance with—Men of Confi-Dance stand out quickly. Not long into the general dance sessions, the bolder ladies began lining up around this entryway to the dance floor, and before a Man of Confi-Dance could take the lady he has just danced with back to the sitting area, one of these barracudas would be asking him for the next dance. It was like running the gauntlet to get out onto the dance floor each time. I may be making these ladies sound terrible, but in reality, they know the ropes at these dance weekends, and they probably enjoy more dancing than ladies not bold enough to go up and ask a man for the next dance. So for a lady reading this, consider the following: Most Men of Confi-Dance are flattered when asked to dance by a lady even if they can't accept that invitation for some reason. These men will usually be polite, thank the lady for asking, and agree to get back with them a little later, perhaps even the next dance. They will not think the lady is being rude, they will not think they are being hit on, they will not think they are obligated to accept, and in most cases, they will end up dancing with that lady either right then or not long afterward.

Over the years of being a dance host and by just meeting ladies at various dance venues, I have been amazed at how many of these ladies have begun ballroom dancing later in life. Many of these ladies are now divorced or widowed and have either read or been told by friends that dancing is a good way to get back into the dating scene or at least a nice way to meet new friends. So many of these ladies have never experienced the sheer enjoyment that ballroom dancing brings to their lives now that they no longer have a significant other who wouldn't dance with them. They have awakened to find a wonderful social activity that is at the same time a physical, enjoyable, and enticing pastime. They meet new friends, both men and women, and become regulars in dance clubs, USA Dance chapters, local lounges, etc.

I know many who have become fanatical about their dancing, taking lesson after lesson, sparing no expense, hungry for progress, and for acknowledgment from their peers. Dancing had been missing from their lives for years, or even forever, and at an older age now, they want to make the most of it. And it hasn't gone unnoticed by them that the other half of the couple dancing is a man! She is going to be in the arms of a gentleman each time she dances, something that she has missed for a long time, and something she finds quite enjoyable and exciting.

MOC escorting ladies to dinner on cruise

I met Cyndi Blindt, a vivacious lady from Huntington Beach, California, and a flight attendant with United Airlines on a Mediterranean cruise recently where I was hosting. She was part of our group and was there with her dance partner, Don Quon, from nearby Irvine, California, who had been retired from Boeing for a year or more. She looked like a real dancer, experienced and confident, and beaming her smiles whenever on the dance floor. I was shocked to find out she had only been dancing for a year and a half. When I asked her when dancing had become important to her, she replied, "It's always been important; I'm Italian, what can I say? We have huge family reunions, most men would play instruments, and we would all dance and dance. And at weddings too, but it was not ballroom dancing, as I do now."

Cyndi told me she had gone on a cruise about eight years ago where there were dance hosts. All the hosts danced with her a lot *(Who wouldn't want to dance with vivacious Cyndi?* I'm thinking), and she loved it and wanted to learn, but it was not the right time in her life. She had to wait some years, and then one of the dance hosts who had kept in touch with her *(Who wouldn't want to keep in touch with vivacious Cyndi?* I'm thinking), finally got her to go to an Argentine tango workshop, and she decided she wanted to learn more. She had a girlfriend who was into country dancing and west coast swing, and they'd go together to singles dances, and they became hooked on dancing.

"I learned a lot of stuff without instruction but seemed to pick it up quite naturally and quickly," Cyndi explained. "Now with my dance partner, Don, I've come a long way. If we go places where they have dancing, like in the tourist area of Athens before this cruise, we can just step up and dance. I was embarrassed like we were putting on a show but because Don was making me look good, I relaxed and began to enjoy it. He was the Man of Confi-Dance that made that good moment happen for the two of us." *(Who wouldn't want to be putting on a show on the street in Athens, Greece, with vivacious Cyndi?* I'm thinking.)

Cyndi wants to look like many of the experienced ladies she sees dancing—she's impatient, she wants to know all the dances and all the steps right now! But this is natural for many women now getting into dancing in a strenuous and dedicated way. At this point in her life, Cyndi wonders, "When will the legs go, when will the hips go, and I want to accomplish more and more in a short time. Anything could happen that could ruin my dancing future, so I want to get in as much as I can."

I told Cyndi, "When a lady I'm dancing with who is relatively new begins making polite excuses that she's new and she doesn't know the pattern, etc., I just tell her, I was there once too. Be patient and just enjoy what you can do now."

Like so many ladies new to the joys of dancing, Cyndi says dance just fills her heart with joy, makes her smile and smile. She wasn't smiling today at anyone in particular, she was just smiling; she was so happy to be dancing and feels there's no better medicine in the whole world for depression or problems or whatever. She truly feels that your mind affects your body, so being upbeat eliminates the negatives and keeps you healthy. Cyndi continues to fill her life with the joy of dancing and hopes her children and grandchildren also will learn the joys of dancing during their lives. It's never too early to learn to dance. (Is there an echo in here? I thought I'd heard that or said that before.)

A man reading this doesn't have to be a college mathematics professor (like I was for a number of years) to figure out that one-half of each couple on a dance floor is a man, and there are ladies lining up everywhere to dance. That means there certainly must be an unfulfilled demand for men who can dance—that's right, a great need for Men of Confi-Dance. The odds are with us guys and all we need to do is learn to dance confidently at least for starters.

In some parts of the country, like in south Florida's east coast, the Men of Confi-Dance are far outnumbered by the available ladies at almost any given dance venue. I attended a dance in the Vero Beach area with my former wife, Linda, while visiting the area several years ago. She and I are still the very best of friends, and the opportunity to join her for an evening of dancing was an invitation I was happy to accept. There must have been two hundred or more people in attendance, but mostly couples, I observed, and mostly of the retirement age. And these ladies with husbands or significant others don't like to play sharesies, which was pretty obvious. Available men are hard to find down there and thus worth fighting to keep, it seemed. I danced with Linda for a number of dances, and then they announced a mixer.

Let me interrupt a moment and point out that at our USA Dance chapter's monthly dances and most other organized ballroom dances I attend, mixers are held once or twice during the afternoon or evening and give those men and women without partners a chance to dance. Normally foxtrots or waltzes are played for a mixer, and a mixer usually incorporates three to four songs in a row. As the ladies lined up on one side of the dance floor, I noticed that the line only had a dozen or less ladies, while the floor filled with couples who did not participate in the mixer. In other words, those ladies with partners were not about to share their partners even for a mixer with the other single, available, and ready ladies in the line. I have always participated in these mixers when I attend dances. I feel it is appropriate for me, even if I am there with a partner, to dance with these ladies during the mixer. Some of these ladies may not be getting asked to dance too often. Besides being the polite thing to do, it also gives me a chance to dance with ladies I either don't know or ladies I hardly dance with. Either way, it always helps me hone my leading skills and helps me feel I have shared my dancing abilities with these appreciative ladies.

So here I am, back in Vero Beach, lining up to dance with the ladies in the mixer, one of the few single gentlemen who either had the interest (or the nerve) to participate. There were not that many ladies in the line, but still they outnumbered the men who were coming up to the line. The second lady I danced around the room was around my age, exquisitely dressed, covered in jewelry, and held on to me fairly tightly. She said she hadn't seen me there before, and I replied that it was my first time and that I was from Lakeland (about two hours away). She smiled sweetly and said that they sure could use another "fine-dancin' man" like me over in their neck of the woods. When I smiled but did not reply, she added, "I'm sure several of us ladies could find a suitable place for you to live over here, if you wanted to."

Man, they don't mess around when it comes to "fine-dancin' men" in South Florida. They truly prove that if "a good man is hard to find," then "a good dancin' man is even harder to find," and they seem quite willing to be accommodating. In some of these areas, for instance, Boca Raton on the east coast and Sarasota on the west coast, a Man of Confi-Dance is often hired by one or more ladies to be their private dance host for the afternoon or evening. If more than one lady goes in together with another lady or two, they just split the cost and split the dancing time. If you think this sounds tacky or improper, consider that these ladies do not have dance partners, want very much to dance, and are willing to pay for a good dance partner (a Man of Confi-Dance, not an escort). Is this any different than their paying for someone to provide any other service needed that they are unable to do themselves, such as landscapers, home repairmen, pool cleaners, personal trainers at the fitness center, auto repairmen, dance instructors, tennis instructors, etc.? The guys who do this type of dance hosting are recognized in their communities as some of the best dancers around, and when they are willing to hire out as dance hosts, it can be a win-win situation all around. A Man of Confi-Dance gets in a good day's (or night's) work dancing, he continues to improve personally while the ladies he dances with usually do the same, he is recognized by others as a Man of Confi-Dance, and he brings home a few extra bucks that he may in turn use with his dance coach for further training.

There was a relatively new dance studio in my town that opened its doors to anyone to participate in their dance night once or twice a month. I went a couple of times when they were first getting started. There were not that many ladies to dance with, and most were beginners. I didn't really enjoy those evenings very much and did not get in very much dancing, and so I haven't been back. Recently, I ran into the owner/instructor and related this to him. I also mentioned that it wasn't worth paying the ten bucks to come and not dance much, but that if he wanted me to attend as a dance host for free, I would like to try that out when I was in town, and he agreed. There is always a place that a Man of Confi-Dance will be appreciated and perhaps rewarded with one benefit or another.

CHAPTER 24

Many Nice Guys Do Finish First

"Dancing with you makes me feel all fluffy,
like I was dancing on a cloud."
—Chris (Liev Schreiber)
Mixed Nuts **(1994)**

ONE OF THE great benefits of being a dance host on a cruise ship is meeting not only many wonderful ladies but meeting the other great dance hosts you work with. Over the years, I've had the privilege of working beside and/or rooming with some excellent fellow dance hosts who each in his own right is a Man of Confi-Dance.

The one I've probably hosted with most is Tom Scheffer, seventy, who is now retired and living near Columbus, Ohio. Tom began at Arthur Murray thirty-five or forty years ago after his divorce. He found himself in a stressful job, single again, and needing to relax and loosen up. In fact, his first teacher would harp on him to unwind. After taking lessons off and on for thirty-five years, Tom said to me about the title of this book, "Confi-Dance is the right word because if you know how to dance, you don't need much else. You don't need to be a conversationalist. Just make the woman you are dancing with as comfortable as possible and show her off to the extent that you can as this is a big plus. You can meet a lot of women through dancing and many good friends too."

Fellow dance host, Tom Scheffer, with Joan Miller

Tom is part of a community of ballroom dancers in Columbus who make it a point to dance with each other's partners too because it is a real social culture there. I've known Tom on many hosting jobs on cruise ships, and Tom is certainly a Man of Confi-Dance who shows the ladies a good time.

"With retirement, you have more time to devote to dancing, and it's a good activity and social venue too," Tom adds. He and his companion and dance partner, Mary Wile, know many dancing friends into their '90s who still get much pleasure from their dancing.

When I asked Tom to recall when he was not a Man of Confi-Dance, he shook his head regretfully and explained, "I was awkward in high school like many other teenagers and stood on the sidelines talking to the other guys—not getting involved in the dancing. I remember the guys who did dance—every woman wanted to be with them, whether they were good or not, because they wanted to be out there dancing and moving. I never did get the message until I was forty-some years old." That's a lot of years for any of us to miss out on the enjoyment we derive from dancing. It's even a lot more years to miss if you're still not dancing.

Tom will tell you, "It's always a high moment to dance with someone at a formal venue or on a cruise ship and have the lady say, 'It's a pleasure to dance with you, and I hope you'll ask me again.' Or doing a cha cha on a village square to the music of a street musician, and have the people clap for you—that takes being a Man of Confi-Dance. Putting that tux or white dinner jacket on and taking a woman out on the floor who looks like a million dollars and to do that with comfort, ease, and grace is definitely a high point." I'll second that—it's exactly what stimulated me to write this book and share these ideas.

Tom and I have remained good friends off the cruise ship too and have enjoyed several weeks of skiing the western slopes together over the past few years. It's a really nice bonus of being a dance host and meeting good friends. We've also shared a beer in many of the great ports around the world, from Tallinn, Estonia to Auckland, New Zealand to Tierra del Fuego, Chile to Buenos Aires, Argentina, and others too numerous to mention in between. He's a consummate gentleman with the ladies and a pleasure to work and room with aboard the cruise ships.

When Tom and Mary visited me in Florida this past year, Mary, sixty-seven, who is from Columbus, Ohio, told me she's been ballroom dancing since 1995, although as a kid and teenager she loved to dance. She has early memories of grade school when they had to take dance lessons, and the boys hated it. They were all too tall or too short. The guys couldn't wait to get out of the class. Junior high was sock hop time when the guys would stand around just staring at the girls who would have no other recourse than to dance with each other. (They didn't get it yet, did they?) One or two guys could dance and were very popular since all the girls wanted to be with them. (Those one or two guys certainly got it.) Had the other guys known, they could have been popular without too much effort.

Mary didn't take ballroom lessons since her husband was not a dancer, so she got along without. Then, in 1995, her nephew, George, came to live with her from Hungary, where he was a competitor in ballroom dancing. He was shy and didn't make friends early on, but on the dance floor he was wonderful. He taught her to dance, and she went to college competitions with him and then to England for more competitions. This is how she began her love of ballroom dance. She owned an art gallery then, and a client came in who danced and offered to trade ballroom lessons for her art, and this is when her dancing really evolved.

Mary remembers when she and Tom were at the Columbus State House in a great room with a marble floor, and she said to Tom, "Wouldn't it be nice to dance in this room?" There was no one there, so they hummed a Viennese waltz and danced around the state house having a wonderful and memorable moment. Then when they were finished they heard applause. They looked up and there were maids on the balcony applauding and smiling, and it made them enjoy their dance that much more. Tom Terrific, the Man of Confi-Dance, was able to make this moment happen for his lady.

Greg Sipe, fifty-nine, from York, Pennsylvania, is a full-time dance instructor and a popular dance host with Dancers at Sea. Greg is someone with whom I've shared a cabin as well as the dance floor, the dinner table, and the ladies on a number of wonderful cruises. He began at twenty-one years old teaching part-time. Greg has a vast background of training with a variety of the real dance masters. He found a dance instructor whom he called the best of the best and trained with her in New York City for three to four years. He finally left his full-time job with ITT a few years later to open his own studio and has been teaching full-time since. He actually began dancing at nineteen because of a girl he wanted to impress, but he never impressed her with dancing, though they are still friends.

Did Greg not impress girls before nineteen? "Perhaps, but I was not confident that I was," says Greg. "I was not a Man of Confi-Dance yet. It can make a difference in your life. 'Dancing mirrors life' and in that way it's a practice zone for living."

I asked Greg if he could recall anyone coming to him for a specific need in dancing, not necessarily to learn a lot of dancing. One man he thinks of (a great surprise to him) called him on a Saturday needing to dance with his daughter at her wedding—within a week! The man came in three times and learned some basic foxtrot without spending much time, just the bare minimum. Greg wondered about him later and received a phone call thanking him, reporting how delighted he was with how it went.

"It might have been the shortest time period that we had to give a man the confidence he needed for a special moment. He appreciated it," said Greg. "There are times when you think back at something that worked out like it did with this person, and you hear back from them with a thank you." He was a Man of Confi-Dance for that one specific moment, thanks to Greg, who shared with me his high moments in life because he is a Man of Confi-Dance. "Being able to dance with your own peers, or with ladies, trainers, or coaches who are better, and feeling that they think just as much of you as you do of them—that makes it worthwhile to work hard. And to just simply go to a wedding and be able to dance with anyone to any music feels special." This seems to be a common theme among men who can dance with confidence.

Greg has a low-key and low-voice style of teaching lessons on our days at sea that gets across what he wants us to learn, usually a pattern or two we can use during the duration of the cruise. He's a great fellow dance host, and I always enjoy working with him on a cruise ship. I hope we'll be sharing the same dance floor again in the future.

Bill Coleman, sixty-nine, a retired interior designer from Palm Beach, Florida, was my roommate on a recent cruise that took in Greece, Turkey, Israel, Egypt, and Italy. He and I never stopped laughing, it seemed, with all the jokes and one-liners we knew and parried back and forth with each other. He is an astute dresser, well-bred, and well-read, and thus always a hit socializing with the ladies in our group. Bill first became a Man of Confi-Dance in junior high as he recalls Friday afternoons when they pulled the tables and chairs back in the cafeteria and had sock hops with jitterbugs. Being as good as his peers, he wasn't afraid to ask the girls to dance and always had a great time.

In later years in the bars of New York City, Bill was never afraid to ask a lady to dance. He kept up with the new dances, like swing, hully gully, and twist during the '60s. Later, he and three of his good friends would go to all of the Palm Beach JC dances where they danced and danced (social dancing, not ballroom dancing). That changed when he was introduced to ballroom dancing by going to social balls in Palm Beach.

"A bit later, I spotted an ad to become a teacher, but I became a dance host instead, for twenty years," Bill told me. "It's the way to travel, to meet people, go places, have fun and adventure, and it's very social. On ships I can ask a lady to dance, and by just taking her hand I can tell what kind of dancer she will be." Like a Man of Confi-Dance should, he will dance her dance level and keep her in time with the music and help her enjoy the dance. He was a close friend of Zsa Zsa Gabor for years, and though "we did a lot of things together, and I went in place of her to Hollywood events at times, we never danced together," Bill recalled. Well it would seem to me that Zsa Zsa lost out here.

On this same cruise mentioned above with Bill as my roommate, we had a third roommate. Whereas Bill and I were the old men of the hosts group, the youngest was Piero della Santina, twenty-six, a personable and talented young ballroom instructor and dance escort from Hollywood, California. When I asked him about being a Man of Confi-Dance, Piero told me he first felt it during his college years in Utah where he studied dance and where dance ability was highly looked upon. In that atmosphere, he matured as a dancer.

"But I wasn't a Man of Confi-Dance back in high school," he confided, "where I was shy and afraid to dance. I had a dance form that the others didn't understand nor appreciate so I didn't dance the way I liked around others. But now I feel confident in my ability to ask any lady to dance wherever dance music is being played. And when I am on cruises like this, I get a personal high when I have danced with a lady, and observers come up to acknowledge what I do for the ladies I dance with." Ladies, make note of what Piero is inferring here: We Men of Confi-Dance do what we can to make dancing fun and enjoyable for the ladies and have a great time ourselves doing just that!

Robert Cooper, from the LA area, has been the pro dance instructor and a fellow dance host on most of the cruises I have done with Dancers at Sea. Robert is a well-trained and excellent teacher and can make any of the ladies in our group look "fabulous" on the dance floor. While he has a large following at his dance studio in California, he still loves to travel, see the

Ed Hale and Tom Scheffer and their ladies

world, and loves being part of the Dancers at Sea group. He has taught not only the ladies in each of our groups many new steps and patterns, he has help me and other fellow dance hosts an enormous amount as well.

Ed Hale is probably as smooth a dancer as you'll see and is always popular as a dance host and helps bring out the best in my dancing when we are working on the same cruise. He is a true gentleman, sharp dresser, always treats the ladies with respect, and never tires in his love of dancing.

Horst Wasserman was a fellow dance host on many of my cruises in the first few years I hosted. While another favorite with the ladies, Horst seems to have an unlimited source of energy and puts as much into the last dance of the evening as he does the first. He was due to be a host on one of the cruises I was on out of Fort Lauderdale once when he forgot to do something to keep his passport current and had to watch us sail out of the port without him. We need to always be on top of the details.

Dale Moreth is another fellow dance host I truly enjoy working with. He can make almost any dance fun, keeps the ladies laughing with his spontaneous and humorous deviation from the normal steps, and pulls it off effortlessly. He's always ready to be part of the fun, both on the giving and on the receiving side. Dale and I were roommates on the South Pacific cruise when Nancy and I reconnected, and we have hosted together several times with Mike and Peg Johnston on their DJ cruises.

My roommate on the Alaskan cruise when Nancy and I first met was Ben Edeling, another California dance instructor and a really nice guy. Ben and I spent the entire week trying to verbally one-up the other and became good friends doing so and still keep in touch. I'm still hoping he is planning to will me the sharp tuxedo shirt with the crossed collars he wore on that cruise that I loved.

Dancing Over the Seven Seas group photo

Richard "Dick" Obney and I have hosted together with Lennie Corbett of Dancing Over the 7 Seas and always have a great time trying to identify the artists of the songs played on the ship's big band channel each night while dressing for the evening's dinner and dancing. Dick was a regional vice president of USA Dance, plus the owner of a company that videos ballroom dance competitions. He invited me to video a few competitions with him in Florida which, I found, takes immense concentration, fast hands, attention to detail, and gave me a new look at the world of competition.

Stan Andrews, the current national secretary of the USA Dance organization and longtime worker with USABDA before that, roomed with me on one of the USABDA sanctioned cruises I hosted. Stan always showed good dance host ethics and dressed the role impeccably.

MOC and fellow dance host, Stan Andrews

RAOUL WEINSTEIN

Another of my favorite fellow dance host is Mario Avila, even another California dance instructor if you can imagine that. Mario is a great dancer, a great host, and a great guy to go ashore with. And he's always "cool." On a Baltic Sea cruise, Mario and I walked miles and miles in Copenhagen, Denmark (the day I had my $12 beer!), Gdansk, Poland, and Tallinn, Estonia. He picked up a hat for a buck at some street flea market in one of the ports and put it together with his outfit that night and wowed everyone. When you're with Mario, there are always going to be good times and good laughs.

RW, Howard Smallowitz, Tom Scheffer, Mario Avila, et al on Med cruise

MOC and Dieter with Tina on formal night

As you can see, what most of us dance hosts share is the love of ballroom dancing, the highs we get making our dancing special and enjoyable for our dance partners, our desire to travel the world and seek the adventure that faraway places bring into your life, the appreciation for the elegant environment that cruise ships afford for an activity that brings us so much pleasure, and the opportunity to meet and make such wonderful friends over the years. What's that? I think I hear the familiar chimes from down the passageway signaling that high tea is now being served on the Upper Promenade Deck. Gotta go now. This really is the life!

RAOUL WEINSTEIN

Section Five

The Dancer's World

IN THE PREVIOUS four sections, I have attempted to illustrate how dancing can be a positive force in enhancing a man's self-esteem, bring happiness to himself and to those in his life, and open potential doors to romance and adventure. But there is much more when you enter the dancer's world. Dancers, and in particular Men of Confi-Dance, should be expected to practice a higher level of etiquette, to properly dress the part, and to exude the appropriate and well-deserved aura. They can take their dance abilities into other areas of their lives with ease and enjoyment. And through their dancing, they often bring change to their lives and to the lives of those close to them.

CHAPTER 25

The Dancers' Rules Of Etiquette

"Want to spend lots of time dancing with ladies?
Impress them with how good they are."
—Gerald Cosby

ONCE YOU BECOME a Man of Confi-Dance, you must become acquainted with and adhere to various rules of etiquette. Although these rules apply to almost any style of dancing, they are particularly important with regard to ballroom dancing.

When you know your stuff and want others to see that you know your stuff, it is easy to showboat during a dance to impress those watching you. While you may think that you are entitled to show off now and then because you are good enough to do so, try thinking of the lady you are showboating with. Maybe she isn't as advanced as you or she's apprehensive that she can't do what you are doing. This may cause her to feel inferior or uncomfortable while you whiz her along through some fancy or intricate set of steps that she probably doesn't know. Your obligation is to dance with her with respect for her well-being and for her feelings during the dance. You must set the standard.

When you are out on the dance floor, be aware of the other dancers around you at all times. When you become a more experienced and more adept dancer than most of the other dancers, this dictates that you should be the one to give the right of way to others who may not be able to maneuver as well as you. This is not just a courteous gesture on your part but comes under the classification of floor craft, and a Man of Confi-Dance should always exhibit this quality as he finesses his way around the line of dance. Other dancers will not only pick up from you how to avoid collisions and getting in the lanes of faster moving couples, but they will also respect you for your ability and willingness to be a courteous leader. There are many men who are very good dancers, and know it, and feel like they own the floor and that everyone else should let them have whatever part of the floor they want. They bull their way around the floor expecting other dancers to give them the right of way. It reminds me of the constant battle on the ski slopes between skiers and snowboarders. The question goes: "What's the first thing a snowboarder will say to a skier on the slopes?" And the answer is, "Sorry, dude."

When you invite a lady to dance, show her respect and be aware of her comfort level. Smile, take control, and lead her through something she can follow easily, so she can quickly gain her composure and her confidence. Assume a face that tells her and tells anyone else watching that you are enjoying this dance (even if you're not), and that you are not embarrassed to be seen with her on the dance floor. This is especially true if she made the invitation to you to dance. A Man of Confi-Dance should be polite and respectful enough at a dance; he should be a *mensch*, especially if he is seen by most to be a good dancer, and to accept, in most cases, an invitation to dance from a lady even if she is not particularly attractive or very good at dancing. She is there to enjoy some dancing, and if she has the *chutzpa* or nerve to ask a good dancer, a man she sees as a Man of Confi-Dance, for a dance, then she deserves to be treated properly and given every opportunity to enjoy this dance. This is not a marriage proposal nor are you committing the rest of your evening to this lady, but you should commit your efforts to making this a good dance for her. Who knows, while you are being a proper gentleman to this lady, it just might be that while she may not be much of a dancer nor much of a looker, her friends just might be, and they may be next in line to ask you once they see how you dance with and treat their friend!

When the dance ends, it is proper to escort the lady back, while holding her arm or hand or placing a hand behind her waist or back, to where you were when you asked her to dance. You should also thank her for the dance even if you did not particularly enjoy the dance or her company. The Man of Confi-Dance should be polite and gentlemanly at all times.

A man must take care of and protect the lady he dances with on the dance floor. Remember the moment in the wonderful Japanese version of *Shall We Dance* when the female dance instructor related a past incident of how she had fallen to the floor in an international competition? After that fall, their partnership was never the same. A Man of Confi-Dance should try to keep her from falling or slipping or from losing her balance during the dance. This can be a real job on a cruise ship, for instance, when the ship is rocking and rolling almost as much as the dancers. It can also be true when the lady is older, or has some physical disability, or is not used to the particular dance you are doing, and perhaps puts a little too much energy into her turns or rotations and needs a strong lead and frame from you to keep her under control, both for the safety of the two of you and for the enjoyment of the dance itself.

Another point of etiquette when approaching a lady to dance is to observe if she is with a male companion. When you ask her to dance, recognition should be made to her companion. For example, "Would you care to dance this waltz with me?" should be followed with directing your attention to her companion and adding, "if you don't mind," or, "with your permission." When my lady, Nancy, and I have been at dances, and I am asked to dance by another lady, she feels a bit of invasion when the lady approaches us yet only directs her attention and invitation to me without any acknowledgment of her presence. When this happens, I always turn to her and ask if she minds. She might say, "Not at all." But she might just as well respond, "Yes. I was planning to dance this waltz with you." It is best to find out your lady's feelings right then, not when you return home!

RW dancing with Nancy on cruise

These issues do come up on a regular basis at dance venues such as USA Dance chapter dances, dance studios, on dance cruises, at dance weekends at hotels and resorts, at dance clubs, at retirement communities, etc. Those of us who love to dance recognize that the others in attendance probably also love to dance. That's why it is important to understand the dynamics of the group around you where you are dancing. Many of the others will be couples, with the implication that they may very well be there to dance with each other and no one else. That is not always true, but it may take time to learn the ropes. It has been my experience with my local USA Dance chapter, and those in the area around us that we often visit, that many of the couples do not mind dancing a few dances with other dance partners than their spouses or significant others and in fact look forward to mixing it up a bit. Remember, most are there to dance, to enjoy dancing, and variety is good not only with the various types of dances but with the various types of dance partners as well. So if you find yourself at a dance venue by yourself, inquire among the local regulars what the proper protocol would be at this dance venue.

Last year, on a weekday evening, I decided to go downtown to a beautiful old building by a lake that had been restored with a wonderful wood dance floor because I had noticed a blurb in the "activities today and tonight" column of our local paper. I needed some physical activity and hadn't danced in several weeks, so I dressed suitably, grabbed my dance shoe bag and went to this dance. When I arrived and paid my entry fee, I saw that everyone there was part of a couple—all of the age of retirement. I waited for a while to see if a single lady would appear, but that did not happen. These couples were there to dance with each other, and not one of those men was going to let his lady approach me for a dance, that was pretty evident. After about forty-five minutes, the lady in charge came over to where I was sitting by myself, apologized for not having any ladies there for me to dance with, offered to refund my entry fee, and I went home frustrated and disappointed. But thankfully this is not the norm.

RAOUL WEINSTEIN

CHAPTER 26

The Aura Of The Man Of Confi-Dance

**"Great dancers aren't great because of their technique;
they are great because of their passion."**
—Anonymous

LET'S LOOK AT the myriad of opportunities for dancing and how the Man of Confi-Dance fits in. If there is dancing going on somewhere, the Man of Confi-Dance is going to be comfortable there, is going to be seen there, and is definitely going to be in demand there.

Whenever there's dancing in a bar, lounge, night club, etc., there will more than likely be a line dance played, something like "The Electric Slide" or the "Neon Lights" waltz line dance. There are numerous line dances, some with a set of moves and patterns styled to a cha cha, waltz, or samba beat. Ladies far outnumber guys on the dance floor when these line dances are played. Why? Because for many ladies, they are there because they love to dance and either have no dance partner with them, or they might be there with some guy who doesn't dance with them, and this is a wonderful opportunity for these ladies to get up and strut their stuff.

I have watched some very sharp ladies with some very sharp moves strut their stuff during line dances, like peacocks preening for potential mates. It has helped me determine where the ladies are in the room who want to dance, and any man should know that these ladies want to dance with a man, not with another woman, nor by themselves. It also gives me a chance to see how the ladies can dance and move. The Man of Confi-Dance should have no problem being a hit with ladies like these and being appreciated for asking them to dance. Another telltale sign is to watch ladies who are sitting or standing around. When they start swaying or moving with the music right in place, that's usually a strong signal that they'd like to be out on the floor dancing, especially if they add a smile to their swaying when you glance over their way.

And once you dance with a lady of your choice, you can be certain that the other ladies will be watching you dance and hoping to be dancing with you before long. I remember being asked to help demonstrate the rumba with a lady dance friend of mine, Gale O'Brien, who was teaching dancing to the sixth graders in one of our local elementary schools. It was fun to help and to see the young students adapt to something new to them, especially the young boys who were very fearful of contact with these young girls. But when Gale and I were demonstrating a step to the students, my Cuban motion must have looked a little too suggestive to them, for we could hear and see some of the girls giggling. My point is this: if the young girls are giggling when they see your dance moves, what might the mature ladies be thinking?

I was on a cruise recently with Nancy for our personal enjoyment, not a working cruise as a dance host. Of course, we were excited about being able to dance with just each other each night. There were several lounges with dance music, and we would dance in whichever one had the type of music that sounded good. We would then walk down to another lounge when the band took a break and look for some good dance music from another band. Not having to dance every dance as I am required to do when dance hosting, I had time during those dances that we sat out to observe the other dancers. On a ten-day cruise, it doesn't take long to know who the other dancers are aboard your cruise. They appeared each night just as we did, sometimes in one lounge, sometimes in another. There were dancers of differing abilities, but what they had in common was their enjoyment of dancing. As I watched the different men lead their partners around, I thought of trying to determine which ones I would call a Man of Confi-Dance. After several days, I realized something important: from the couple who had had much training and could put on a showcase if asked, right down to some stumblers who didn't exhibit much in the way of structured ballroom dance steps or patterns, each of these men was, in his own way, a Man of Confi-Dance. Why? Because each one was willing and confident enough to take his lady onto the dance floor and create a moment they could both enjoy. With the exception of the first couple mentioned above, I believe Nancy and I were the next best. Often during that cruise, we noticed that whichever couple, they or us, that took the floor first and began a nice pattern, the other couple would usually opt to sit out, either because they want to let the other have the spotlight or because they did not want to compete on the floor at the same time.

It is never my intent to hog the floor or make others feel like they should not come onto the dance floor when I am there first, but when it does happen that way, a Man of Confi-Dance does indeed take full advantage of having plenty of space and can dance some patterns that are not easily done when the floor is crowded. Nancy was very pleased and enjoyed being complimented often during the cruise by other passengers that had watched us dancing the night away each night.

Another important point to make here: television ads for many medical products or retirement communities or male potency prescriptions such as Viagra and Levitra and Cialis are incorporating scenes with senior citizens dancing and enjoying being involved with dancing. Are they telling us that dancing is just for the senior citizens? Are they telling us that these products are good for dancing? It seems to me they are showing dancing among seniors as a natural and fun way for these older members of our society to stay young, to stay sexy, to stay attractive to the opposite sex, and I'm thinking there's a lesson to be learned here. If a man has decided he doesn't need to be a good dancer or a Man of Confi-Dance to be sexy, and thus hasn't bothered to learn to dance, he may think that he is really not missing out on anything by not being a dancer. And that's okay for now. But when you look at these ads and think of yourself being in a retirement home, or even later, in a nursing home one day, all that you knew about being sexy including how sexy you might have been once might not be of much use to you anymore. However, a Man of Confi-Dance will always be attractive and in demand at whatever age, as long as he is still physically capable of dancing and enjoying the closeness that dancing brings to him and his partner. (See Appendix B for more information on the health benefits of dancing.)

I picked up a recent copy of my AARP magazine, finding a reference to their website picturing a couple in formal wear dancing, with a caption of "Dance Till You Drop." The description below says "Be it ballroom, salsa, or hip-hop, dancing helps lower your cholesterol and blood sugar levels and can also build your immunity and stave off dementia." You are then invited to learn how you "boogie your way to a healthier and longer life." Next thing you know, they will be bottling dancing and selling it on TV along with a set of steak knives as a promotional.

And finally, even the cartoonists for the long-running newspaper comic strip *Mary Worth* must think dancing is the most proper setting for a marriage proposal. In a recent Sunday strip, there is the venerable Mary Worth (didn't I use to follow Mary as far back as the '50s?) in the arms of a smiling gentleman on the dance floor being asked to marry him. At any age, romance still runs rampant on the dance floor, real and fictitious alike.

CHAPTER 27

A Good Chapter In A Dancer's Life

**"The truest expression of a people is in its dance
and in its music. Bodies never lie."
—Agnes de Mille**

MY LONGTIME USA Dance chapter, the Heart of Florida chapter, holds a monthly dance the first Sunday of each month from 3:00 to 6:00 p.m.. My new USA Dance chapter, South Carolina—Upstate, holds its monthly dance the first Saturday night of the month. The goal of any USA Dance chapter is to promote ballroom dancing. This means offering the opportunity to have a dance venue, keeping members informed of these dances plus opportunities to dance elsewhere in our area, seeking new members, playing the best dance music around, having dance lessons at each of our dances, and anything else that keeps dancers happy, connected, and on the dance floor.

I have been a member of the Heart of Florida chapter for probably eighteen years and served a term as chapter president. We are fortunate to have a competent, dedicated, and energetic Heart of Florida chapter president serving her third or fourth term in a row: Terri Lynn Goodrich, fifty-six, from our county seat, Bartow, Florida, and a travel agent for twenty-two years. She has been a dancer for many years, deciding to get involved after she went to the recital of a travel client and watched this seventy-eight-year-old woman dancing a samba. According to Terri Lynn, "I knew that was something I wanted to do." Then she married a man who used to teach dancing and enjoyed being on the dance floor with him.

Terri Lynn began to notice ads and notices for dance cruises and thought that she could do that. Do what? Well, once a year she hosts and organizes a ballroom dance cruise for Mike and Peg Johnston, competitive dancers from the Tampa area and DJs at most of the local competitions and at several ballrooms. She points at me as she says, "There is a need for gentleman dancers of all ages. Women dig guys who can dance."

Terri Lynn's initial experience with dance hosts (she just completed her seventh cruise where I was one of the dance hosts again) was relying on the ladies that had been on other dance cruises to suggest names for hosts. Now she has what she affectionately calls her stable of dance hosts, some from the beginning, some several times. I am happy to be one of the "hosses" in that stable.

One year, there were six of us dance hosts, with me being the only one not a dance instructor. It was a privilege to be working with that caliber of dance talent and hanging in there with them helped assure me the feeling of being a Man of Confi-Dance. "Finding good hosts is very important because I expect the hosts to enjoy dancing even after the scheduled dance times. They love to dance, and the women love to be danced with anywhere, anytime there's dancing available," Terri Lynn points out. "To dance with someone whom you have no interest in takes special skills. Good dance hosts can do this. More and more practice makes everyone better. Ladies enjoy dancing and whether it is the best dance they ever had or not, they get something from it, they learn, they get better at following the lead, and it builds confidence on both sides." She once called me, "the best dance host I have ever had on my dance cruises, without a doubt." I humbly accepted her gracious comment and consider this one of the nicest compliments I've received and one that I try not to take for granted.

Terri Lynn feels that personal relationships are something that we can dance around. She's had her challenges relationship-wise, like the void left when her significant other and dance partner left her life. Then you can't enjoy functions with dancing. (I can certainly relate to that!) After she sat in her own pity party, she re-involved herself again, not only by working hard to make our chapter grow better and better, but she now has a man back in her life that is working on dancing, and she is happy again. Terri Lynn is always a fun person to be around, but a happy Terri Lynn is really something special!

A lot of dancers who are members of USA Dance chapters gradually learn about the other chapters in their area and sometimes chapters in other parts of the country. When I am going to be in another area for more than a few days, I will go on the USA Dance website, www.usadance.org, to find other chapters in that area who might be holding some form of dancing event during my stay there. Several times, including New Year's Eve with Nancy last year, I have located chapter dances where I could go with or without a dance partner and enjoy an afternoon or evening of ballroom dancing. Our Heart of Florida chapter supports, and is supported by, chapters in and around central Florida. This builds a comfortable dance family that you see at dances again and again and makes for a full afternoon or evening of dancing when I do not have a dance partner with me. For information on joining a USA Dance chapter, visit the website or call 1-800-447-9047.

Raoul and Nancy at Georgia Dance Chapter's NYr's Eve Ball

I mentioned my friend, Dean Cooke, sixty-eight, from the Charleston, South Carolina community earlier when I described being an outsider one night at a shag roadhouse. Dean's the kind of guy who will drive great distances to get in some good dancing, seeking potential dance partners far and wide. And Dean is a Man of Confi-Dance.

"I do enjoy dancing," Dean says, "because it provides a wholesome activity, social interaction, physical maintenance, and I look forward to it. It gives me an opportunity to exhibit a creative and artistic part of me."

I asked Dean to tell me about this "creative and artistic part" lurking beneath the surface. Dean explains, "I enjoy dancing with the right partner, where I am extremely proud of what we can exhibit on the dance floor. On a cruise recently on the *Queen Victoria*, on the first day aboard I had the opportunity to dance a rumba with an extremely accomplished ballroom dancer that I had never seen before, and during that rumba, she and I had chemistry. We received compliments throughout the whole cruise from people that had seen us, who wanted to share their appreciation for what they had seen in that one dance. We brought out the best in each other."

Dean has been into ballroom dancing for fourteen years, but before, dancing was not very convenient nor did he have much opportunity. In high school he was one of the guys having a great time dancing what his peers could do. He told me with a slow but forceful discourse that, "Dancing is one thing that you can take with you wherever you go. Nobody can take it away from you in a lawsuit, not the IRS, and not through divorce; it's yours forever. Wherever you go, you have friends as soon as they see that you can dance."

I didn't know Dean could wax so profoundly but he is right on. He has visited USA Dance events all across the USA. "It doesn't take long to receive the warmth and friendship of those that enjoy dancing, and the camaraderie we dancers share is great," Dean added. Some advice Dean has for other current or potential ballroom dancers: "You will need determination if you want to learn to dance because you will be humbled. You will have your good days and your bad days. Take lessons at least twice a week." It's always good to see dancing through the eyes of another Man of Confi-Dance.

Having just relocated to Greenville, South Carolina and having just switched my USA Dance membership to the SC-Upstate chapter, I have gotten to appreciate the fine efforts of Susan Johnson, the president of the chapter but also the district representative for the Carolinas to the USA Dance organization. I have just been invited to join their board. I'm now looking forward to another good chapter in my dancing life.

CHAPTER 28

Combining Dance With Career And Travel Can Be Fun

"To dance is to be out of yourself. Larger, more beautiful, more powerful. This is power, it is glory on earth and it is yours for the taking."

—Anonymous

WHEN I RETIRED several years ago, I had been a real estate agent or broker since the late seventies, beginning this career in St Thomas, Virgin Islands, and continuing when I moved to Florida in the early eighties. In 1999, I was elected President of the Lakeland (Florida) Association of Realtors. Installation of officers was always a very nice affair, usually held at a luncheon or dinner at the prestigious Lakeland Yacht Club on Lake Hollingsworth across from the campus of Florida Southern College. I had attended my share of these events over the years, and decided I wanted to do something a little more dramatic but fun at my installation.

I had been taking lessons in ballroom dancing for several years (maybe six or seven) at this point and decided to use my ability to ballroom dance to highlight my installation as their new president. Fortunately there was a nice parquet wood dance floor in the middle of the large dining room where the luncheon was held. Minutes before our association's executive officer was to call all of the incoming officers to come up to the front to be sworn in, I exited a side door, went into the adjoining men's room where I had a change of clothes waiting, and slipped back into the dining room just as they called my name. I joined the other incoming officers who were all dressed appropriately. I had worn a coat and tie before my quick change, and now I was wearing rags. Literally! People looked over at me wondering what was going on, but I just recited the swearing in word for word along with the others. Then the others were excused, and I was invited to the podium to deliver the incoming president's address.

I smiled and pointed to my outfit, warning my fellow Realtors that we could all be dressing like this if we didn't adjust and get in line with the new technology sweeping through the real estate profession, plus a few other comments in the same vein. Then I implied that I didn't want to be dressed this way, but dressed up fancy like maybe Fred Astaire or Cary Grant or my fellow Realtor Joe Lorio (always dressed impeccably). Joe immediately stood up and announced from the audience, "I can help you with that." Then he and his lady friend and another Realtor came up from the audience, brought out a set of clothes that had been hanging behind a room divider panel. They stripped me down to my boxer shorts and redressed me with my tailcoat tuxedo outfit that I used from time to time for ballroom dance competitions.

When this was accomplished, I thanked them, told the audience that this was more like it that a guy dressed like this really felt good, felt successful, felt like he was ready to just get out and dance. At which time my dance instructor, Mary Dague, stood up in the audience stating, "I can help you with that."

I met her halfway, right on the dance floor, and our emcee then announced eight dances one by one that we exhibited for perhaps a minute each. Half were smooth and half were Latin/rhythm. The audience enjoyed it, I enjoyed it, and after thanking Mary, I went back to the mic and tied it all together. I told them that although I may have appeared to be leading Mary in our dances, she was as much a part of whatever we accomplished on the dance floor as I was, and perhaps even more. I stated that as president of the Lakeland Association of Realtors, I might be the leader, but we were all in it together for the next year, and if we wanted to waltz our way through a successful year, we all had to take a part in accomplishing this goal.

It's really fun to have the opportunity to mix your nonworking interests and hobbies in with your working life when it can be entertaining or a good fit. The Lakeland Association of Realtors also had a custom of holding an annual luncheon to honor the secretaries of the various real estate offices. This was always a fun event because several of our Realtors always organized a great entertainment gig by using a number of the Realtors to act or sing or dance or just let their hair down and have fun. One year I was asked to model some sport coats for a local clothing store. One year I was dressed as Sonny and paired with another Realtor dressed as Cher (we really did look a lot like them) to lip-synch "I've Got You Babe." I helped choreograph a little routine for the two of us to dance and sway through, and we had a good time with it.

Just as I was retiring from being an active Realtor, the group organizing this event asked if I would dance with my current lady in a skit they were putting together called "*Dancing with the Stars* Meets *American Idol.*" We were to do a hot rumba, dressed up for the event, and let the judges have at us. Well, I have to point out here that this lady was more than twenty years younger than me and looked it too. She played well to the audience, and we did a good job trying to do a real rumba as the other couples, not particularly adept at ballroom dancing, were hamming up their dances for maximum applause. The three members playing the judges were good, but what got me was the guy playing Simon. While giving us a good score, he kept up with the persona of Simon and cut me to the quick by adding, "Thanks for the best father-and-daughter act in the show!"

The best father and daughter act in the show

I have had the good fortune to meet some fine people through dancing and dance hosting. My partner in the skit above and I were hosted in California for several days by one of my favorite dancers on several cruises, Joan Miller, of Los Gatos, California. We went with her to her local ballroom for a dance and met many other good dancers. Then Joan let us use her condo on the coast for a few days, making it a great vacation.

Joan told me not long ago that meeting me and dancing with me on various dance cruises had been highlights for her when it came to dancing. This is what a dance host wants to hear, of course, and I think that it goes both ways with Joan. I consider her one of the best dancers of all the ladies whom I've danced with over the years as a dance host. But Joan also has been a superb companion to go ashore and see the sites with me on excursions. We have danced on the shores of New Zealand, the town squares in Vietnam, the sidewalks of European cities, and probably on the beaches of several Caribbean islands.

Joan began dancing about eighteen years ago, although she did recall doing a little jitterbug back in high school. Ballroom dancing began right after becoming divorced, like so many other ladies I have met and with whom I have talked. What does dancing give her? I asked.

Joan replied, "Like hiking, dancing is good exercise, you meet many nice people, and I like the music too." She added, "A Man of Confi-Dance, like you, Raoul, always seems to have a variety of interesting patterns."

Dance time on board with Joan Miller

I smiled, not only for the compliment, but because Joan Miller is always trying to show me more patterns, those that she has learned at her home dance studios. Joan still dances three nights a week and stays active in the group lessons that are available where she dances, mostly at the Starlight, now called the Cheryl Burke Dance Center, due to the *Dancing with the Stars* professional taking a financial position in this popular California studio.

Last fall, I was touring out West with Nancy checking out several ski resorts during their off-season. As a ski trip leader for the past seventeen years, Fitz Rawls, head of the ski department at Bowen Travel Agency in Tampa, scored us some complimentary nights. Knowing that we'd be staying in Big Sky, Montana, for several nights, I e-mailed a lady from that area whom I had met the previous year on a cruise in the Orient. Who would believe that there would be a formal ballroom dance within forty-five minutes of where we were staying one of the nights we'd be there? So we packed tuxedo and evening gown with us, met up with her and her companion, and danced the night away in the mountains of Montana.

This past summer, Nancy and I cruised the Mediterranean and capped our European trip with several days in the Provence region of France at the invitation of Karen Doyle, whom we had met the previous summer on a dance cruise in the British Isles on Cunard's exquisite ship, the *Queen Victoria*.

Karen, sixty-nine, lives in a Sonoma, California, condo half of the year and has a home in Dauphin, France, where she spends the other half of the year. We were lucky in our timing to have the opportunity to enjoy Karen's hospitality for three days. Sitting out on her rooftop patio with a chilled aperitif in hand overlooking the orange-and-red tiled roofs of the homes of this fifteenth-century hilltop village in the rolling hills of Provence, I learned of Karen's dancing background.

Karen Doyle with Nancy in Provence, France

"I've never taken many lessons, but I've loved to dance my whole life," Karen told me. "My parents would put the records on and dance when I was little, and I'd dance around with them. So I'm used to seeing people dance.

"I took ballet through college age and always loved ballroom dancing it seemed," she recalled. "I love music, I love to dance." She was never a fad dancer—strictly ballroom (sounds like an idea for a movie title, right?) She has had dance partners briefly, not professionally, who really liked to dance. She has convinced many men to start dancing and has certainly run across Men of Confi-Dance. A friend told her recently that he loves West Coast swing and attributes it to her getting him started in ballroom dancing.

"A lot of men are reluctant to dance," Karen points out, "but if I'm dating someone who doesn't dance, he will usually try it for me, and most of the time, he will like it." (Ladies, we may need to get Karen's phone number available if you are having trouble getting your man to take lessons!) She'll go to dances where there may not be many available partners, but she always hopes that a really good dancer will appear who will dance with her like she had once on New Year's Eve at the Avalon Ballroom in Catalina,

California. While I always love talking to anyone about dancing, it was so extra special to be talking to Karen about dancing in her beautiful old village in Dauphin, Provence, France.

Ballroom dancers can be a wonderful group of people to meet in your home area as well as all over the world. They can also become lifelong friends. We all share the love of dance and will seek out the opportunity to dance whenever and wherever we can find it. I would bet the same is just as true for dancers of other styles like round dancers, square dancers, tap dancers, ballet and jazz dancers, and others who have a passion for what they love to do. A Man of Confi-Dance in any of these venues will always be welcome and be comfortable in the midst of his kind of dance activity anywhere. Maybe even having to dance with a fine looker like the one below:

MOC, aka Tootsie, on Halloween

RAOUL WEINSTEIN

CHAPTER 29

Competitions: The Path To Fortune, Fame, And Focus

"When you do dance, I wish you a wave o' the sea,
that you might ever do nothing but that."
—William Shakespeare

COMPETITION IS A great way to significantly improve your ballroom dancing. Sometime during the first couple of years of taking lessons with Susan while we were married, the two of us became aware of competitions being held by local chapters of USABDA, including the one in my home area. Some of the other people who were taking lessons from our instructor, Mary, were preparing for competitions, and we went to watch when the competition took place. It was exciting to observe the different levels of expertise, and we decided we'd like to try it too.

This opens a whole new vista for dancers still new to ballroom dancing. It means taking numerous lessons to hone your basic skills, learning interesting patterns and routines in the various dances such as rumba, swing, waltz, etc., and understanding how competitions work. Mary brought us along slowly but surely until we were ready (we thought) for our first competition.

It was held in Tampa by the local Southern Star USABDA chapter. We were entered in the Newcomers Division, plus the Bronze Level of competition. Preparing for competition does have the benefit of making you focus on the task at hand. You really do get into it with all the practice it requires. We were competing in both the smooth and Latin/rhythm divisions. This means two separate styles of dancing: in the smooth division, we needed to be prepared to do a waltz, a foxtrot, and a tango; in the Latin division, we performed a swing, a cha cha, and a rumba.

This also means two sets of costumes or styles of dress for the two separate divisions. Hey, if you're going to compete, you might as well look the part. I wore my dad's old tuxedo for the smooth portion of the competition. Since he and my mom liked to dance, it seemed right to compete in his old tux, which fit me with no alterations needed. Then I would change into black slacks and a blousy, black, satin shirt for the Latin portion. Susan had her outfits to match, of course. She didn't have a fancy expensive competition gown but managed to make one of her nice party dresses fill the bill for the smooth dances, while piecing together a tight tank top and short tight skirt for the Latin/rhythm dances. Many ladies will make do with what they can make work or borrow until they decide that they want to do much more competing, and then they get serious about their gowns and sleek sexy outfits.

It makes no difference how much we practiced and prepared for this first event. We still were not prepared for the instant stress and strain we placed on ourselves when our first heat was called. "Heat 21, Newcomers Smooth—couples 12, 14, 19, and 24 please take the floor." Pause . . . then we walked boldly out onto the dance floor on wooden legs and churning guts. We took our positions, and then we heard: "Dancers, please show us your foxtrot." The music started, and I hoped I also would start and my legs also would work. I tried to keep my arms at the right height, I tried to remember the opening steps I was supposed to take, I tried to take Susan with me, but after a few steps I realized that we had just taken twelve or fifteen steps (a routine that took only four weeks of practice to learn), and now I had to transition into the second pattern. My heart was beating like a bass drum in my chest, and then it hit me—I hadn't taken a breath since the music started. So I gulped a lungful of air, tried to maintain some semblance of a smile, and moved through the remaining patterns we had rehearsed until the music stopped thankfully (after 40 to 60 of the slowest moving seconds you will ever encounter in your life) and the announcer said, "Thank you, dancers." I took Susan's hand, ready to walk off the floor, when I heard the announcer's words, "Dancers, please show us your waltz." Oh yeah, we had to do our waltz and then our tango during this heat.

And then it began again, but this time we were a little readier, and a little less timid, and a little more experienced with one dance already under our belt. So we did our waltz, then our tango, then we exited the floor and sat down. Mary came over and congratulated us on our first-ever heat in the world of amateur ballroom dance competition. We are on the path finally to fortune and fame! We waited about fifteen minutes, and then we repeated the same patterns in the same three dances, but this time we were in the bronze heat of the smooth division, and our competition was a lot more experienced than the ones in the Newcomer division.

After several heats in the smooth portion of the competition, the morning agenda is finished, the judges prepared their results, and places are announced and medals, ribbons, or trophies are handed out for each heat. We garnered a third place here, and a fourth place there, and maybe even a second-place finish *(must have been that heat with only the one other couple, I thought)*. Well, so much for fortune and fame. Finally there was a lunch break where I found that I was famished, having competed on pure adrenalin all morning.

So I ate everything that was available within reach, changed into my Latin clothes, and practiced a bit for the afternoon Latin/rhythm portion. We did our rumba, our cha cha, and our swing routines (learned and practiced for the preceding three to four months), and finally it was all over. At this time, all places having been announced, all prizes having been handed out, and many of the competitors having changed back into street clothes; we all shook hands, sipped a glass of wine, nibbled on some snacks, and we're all one big happy family, we competitors are, including the ones that stared us down in the heat with the tango, or the ones that bumped into us in the swing and made me think it was my fault.

But we had now passed through a new portal, we had been tested under fire, and we had survived. We are no longer just ballroom dancers, we are now competitors in the world of ballroom dancing. We have the ribbons to prove it. We can stand around and actually talk the talk to the other competitors, even those in the silver or gold levels, about future comps, when and where they are being held, and those that might be fun to sign up for. We gush with our praise over the wonderful routines we saw others do and how we wish that one day we will be able to dance like that. And if you do stick with it, that one day will become a reality.

To be sure, the point here is not to claim that it takes competition to make one a Man of Confi-Dance. But it certainly won't hurt because competing is one great way to get better and better and to gain more confidence in your ability to lead properly in most any dance that would come your way. During my years of competition, I would not say I was truly a Man of Confi-Dance yet. There was a year after Susan and I had divorced that I competed in the senior division of some local USABDA competitions and some Senior Games in my county. I danced with several partners in these senior comps and did quite well in my age bracket. In truth, the competition in my division was not that intense. But the bottom line was that for these ladies I competed with, ladies without regular dance partners, I was the Man of Confi-Dance they each needed during those comps, and I was proud and happy to help them (and me) achieve a certain degree of success. At a local dance following one on those comps, I even presented each of the three ladies I had partnered with in the comp a rose—a gesture easily accomplished by any man, much less a Man of Confi-Dance. Hey, Dieter, sometimes I have some class too!

Watching *Dancing with the Stars* whenever I can, I often recall my competitive years. I am normally impressed with what the stars can accomplish with a week's worth of training with their pros. I am convinced that they are really not learning how to do the specific dances they perform that week, like the rumba or quickstep, for instance, but instead learning a comprehensive choreographed routine that will please the TV viewers, the live audience, and hopefully the judges. I am just as certain that if I were ever in a position to ask one of the female stars in the competition to dance a rumba, or a quickstep (if, say, one of these had been the dance performed on that given evening), they would have a tough time following a presentable or even representative version of that dance with me.

Don't get me wrong, as I stated above, the stars do a great job with the time they have to prepare for each week's challenge, but I don't think they become ballroom dancers by being on that show. On the other hand, it sure would be a thrill just to be on that show, and I can believe each one when they say they are really intent on winning and doing their best. And it's hard to say enough about the pros. They are handsome, gorgeous, and athletic, and they are very, very good. While I concentrate on the stars to personally judge them from what I can see they are doing, I also love watching the pros to see if I can pick up any moves or styling or patterns that I can learn and use in my future dancing.

In this chapter, I have mentioned the competition we all can view on TV's *Dancing with the Stars* and the USA Dance level competitions I have been involved with over the years. The stars tell us week after week how much they enjoy being part of this competition, how it is unlike anything else they have ever tried, how hard it is, how gratifying it is, and how much they want to remain in the competition. I believe them. I also believe, as I have said earlier, that they will not walk away from the show with a lot of useful ballroom dance skills that they can use in the future. They are being trained to do a choreographed routine designed to wow the audience and the judges without really learning the true basics of the actual dances they are performing. How can you in one week?

On the other hand, the competitions I have entered, even at the newcomer and bronze levels, are all based on learning the basics of those dances we will perform. There is no question that we will never look one iota as good as the stars with their professional on *DWTS*, and our routines will look dismal in comparison; the difference is that we will have learned the basics of the foxtrot, for example, and the routine in the rumba, for example, will employ bronze level patterns throughout and will be of use to us every time we step on the dance floor for the coming years (as long as we continue to use them and keep in practice). And you will find that you will use these skills with other dancers as well as your own partner as this training is quite universal among ballroom dancers. The focus you will achieve in this basic training will be the foundation upon which to build everything you will want to learn in the future.

That being said and with my noble defense of the lessons and focus and practice and sweat and frustration, etc., incurred in my preparation for these lower level competitions laid out before you, I still would love to be a competitor on *DWTS* one day, even with all its avowed decadence (wink!)

RW and Barb dressed for competition

CHAPTER 30

To Walk The Walk, You've Got To Look The Look

"The dancer's body is simply the luminous manifestation of the soul."
—Isadora Duncan

DRESSING PROPERLY FOR ballroom dancing is not only an art but is important for comfort and safety as well. Since you dance with your feet, we might as well begin with shoes for dancing. Most ballroom dancing (and recreational dancing for the most part too) is done on wood floors. Dance shoes made for and sold to serious dancers have soles and heels of suede leather that help you move across the floor smoothly and effortlessly. Dancers will carry their dance shoes in a shoe bag to and from the dances, putting them on when they are at a table or in chairs on or near the wooden dance floor, and removing them and changing back to their street shoes before leaving the floor so as not to ruin these shoes on rough and/or dirty or wet surfaces.

When you are going out to a lounge, a club, a dance for a charity, or to a social event, you may not know what type of floor you will find for dancing. You might bring your dance shoes, but you may not wear them if the floor is not wooden for instance. And for a night of clubbing or for an unexpected opportunity somewhere to jump up and dance, you probably wouldn't have toted your dance shoe bag along anyway. Dress or even smart casual shoes with leather soles and heels will usually be all you need for some casual dancing. But if you end up dancing nonstop for hours, these shoes might wear blisters or sore spots on your feet, and if you are dancing on rough concrete like at a street dance, you might wear down a good pair of leather soled loafers in no time.

While rubber-soled shoes are more comfortable for walking, they are not good for dancing. They will not allow you to turn or pivot as they grip the floor unlike the smooth leather-soled dance shoes and can be a strain on your knees. That will greatly limit the patterns and steps you will be able to use, and you will rarely look like a Man of Confi-Dance with those shoes on. However, there is always a moment for the Man of Confi-Dance to make a lady feel wonderful in whatever shoes he is wearing (maybe even bare feet on the sand) when the time and place is just right for a spontaneous or impromptu dance, even if for as little as a fleeting twenty seconds.

As for your dancing clothes, just because you plan to dance at the venue you are attending does not mean that you will dress that much differently than the dress code suggested for everyone else. If it's a formal affair, you should certainly dress in a formal outfit. If it's a coat and tie event, wear your coat and tie or a suit. If it's a smart casual event, dress appropriately. Just realize that if you plan to dance a good bit, you need for your clothes to feel comfortable and to allow you the range of movement needed to execute the various steps and moves you will want to employ. I wear dress slacks that look good, but some are tighter than others and even with the proper belt worn, I will often find myself having to tug my pants up a bit as they might slide down slightly after a fast swing or saucy cha cha. The same can happen with your socks if they do not have enough elasticity to hold on to your calves and not slide down.

Shirts also need some attention. When dressing smart casual, for example, which is the dress code on many nights on a cruise, if you are planning to spend sometime on the dance floor, wear a shirt that makes you look like a dancer without making it obvious. I like to wear collarless shirts that are full with somewhat fluffy sleeves. I have these shirts in black, white, gold, metallic gold, red, and a few collared shirts that still have some pizzazz. When not on the dance floor, say at dinner or at a cocktail hour, they do not necessarily telegraph that you are a dancer but look sporty enough to fit in nicely. But when you take the dance floor as a Man of Confi-Dance, this look will enhance your appearance and add to your performance and your aura. It is also good practice to wear a sleeved or sleeveless undershirt under your dance shirt to keep perspiration from showing through.

Since this book is dedicated to helping male readers become Men of Confi-Dance, it is not aimed at what a lady should wear for dancing. Ladies who dance a lot will certainly learn what works and what does not work for them on the dance floor. The Man of Confi-Dance however must be perceptive enough to know when the dress a lady is wearing might prohibit some moves or steps in certain dances. For instance, a lady in a sheathlike dress will not be able to follow a corte lead in the tango and look rather clumsy trying to do one. Be wary too of dresses with billowing sleeves as you will find yourself getting your right hand tangled up behind her left shoulder when bringing her back into closed position in many dances. Also dresses with layers around the shoulders and back can trap your right hand in the same way, and sometimes you find yourself sliding your right hand behind her left shoulder as you bring her toward you, only to find that your hand is actually underneath her dress and against her bra strap, camisole, or perhaps even bare skin. If you find yourself dancing with a lady with a dress or outfit like this, just do your best to lead her properly, and if your hand snags on her dress, let her know politely. But do not offer to help her into another dress more suitable for dancing!

Ladies who wear fancy rings with big stones when dancing can create a hazard for a man's hand in a fast dance like swing or jive, especially if those rings have sharp edges. These can just as easily turn sideways on the lady's finger and cause her pain if caught between her fingers when the man takes her hand. If a lady is not wearing appropriate shoes for ballroom dancing, you are both in big trouble, especially if her shoes are rubber-soled. She will be unable to complete a simple underarm turn in any dance and limit you to just a few basic and boring steps all evening.

I've danced with ladies with rubber-soled shoes, and an eight-minute cha cha in a lounge with this lady is not much different from a life sentence in Folsom Prison and will turn you off dancing for the rest of the evening. I have danced with ladies with flimsy backed dresses (like those mentioned above) where my hand was playing hide and seek with her dress or her back during the entire dance. I have cut my fingers on the rings of ladies in fast dances. I have had my glasses knocked off many times by wild elbows from ladies doing an underarm turn in a fast swing or cha cha. I have had my foot stepped on many a time by a lady who should have been using her "other right foot" instead of her right foot. I have fallen down when my partner lost her balance and hung on to me too long. And I have had my face whiplashed by a lady's ponytail in the swing on more than one occasion. Vince Lombardi, the immortal coach of the Green Bay Packers for many years, once stated: "Football is not a contact sport. Football is a collision sport. Dancing is a contact sport." But it's the kind of contact I like, and I would never stop dancing and enjoying the sheer rapture and the sense of accomplishment when a lady I'm dancing with and I really connect on the dance floor and do it right. That is the ultimate true pleasure of being a Man of Confi-Dance. Looking the part just makes it that much better.

MOC at bar of cruise ship

CHAPTER 31

Life Is A Dance, So Dance For Life

"Dance Me to the End of Love"
—Song by Leonard Cohen

"I HAVE SOMETHING I can take with me for the rest of my life," said an outgoing star after being voted off TV's *Dancing with the Stars*. It was the experience of a lifetime for her, she implied, and though disappointed by not being able to continue, she was happy she had had this opportunity to learn some wonderful dance routines and appear on live television. And those of us watching certainly would hope we could have the same chance one day.

Most of us will not get that chance to be either a star or a professional appearing on *Dancing with the Stars*. But that doesn't mean that anyone reading this book can't find something from dancing that will stay with them for the rest of their life. Within the lyrics of the wonderful song by Leonard Cohen, "Dance Me to the End of Love," you will find these beautiful and deeply personal longings expressed:

> *"Dance me to the wedding now, dance me on and on,*
> *Dance me very tenderly and dance me very long,"*

And also,

> *"Dance me to the children who are asking to be born."*

There is symmetry of dancing and life—they are truly symbiotic. Weddings are for dancing, for expressing our joy and happiness at this wondrous event, and we should all take part in the celebration. Dance with your daughter, dance with your wife, dance and smile and let the pleasure fill you.

Dance on and on. Make dancing a part of your life for the rest of your life. It will bring you so many wonderful moments that are being shared with your partner(s). Dance tenderly, dance wildly, dance with classy elegance, dance with fervor, dance with your heart, dance by yourself, or dance with a partner, but dance.

I do not know exactly the meaning Leonard Cohen had in mind when he wrote the lyrics, "Dance me to the children who are asking to be born." But it stirs in me a feeling of continuity, of legacy-building from generation to generation. Men have danced since time began, and their acts have been passed down over the years. However, in modern times, the art and joy of dancing is not always passed down from father to son, and if you did not inherit the love and artistry of dancing from your parents, I urge you to learn it now so you can pass it on to "the children who are asking to be born" in your life if not born already.

By now you have read my story. You have seen how dancing came into my life and stayed. You know the exciting places where dancing has taken me, and the wonderful people I have met through dancing, right up to and including, Nancy, the special lady and partner in my life and now my fiancée. I have shared all of this with you for a reason: to passionately encourage you to bring dancing into your life, or if it is there already, to make it more meaningful and exciting for you and the people close to you. I have told you that you can make this happen for one special moment in your life or for the remaining years of your life. As the TV star I quoted above felt, make some momentous experience (or perhaps a lifetime) of dancing be something you can take with you for the rest of your life. And at the same time, make your dancing something that one of or more of your partners can take with them for the rest of their life too.

So here it is one last time: it is never too early or too late in your life to learn to dance well enough to bring some joy and excitement into your life and to those around you. The number 1 *New York Times* best-selling author Nelson DeMille wrote in his sharp fast-paced novel *The Gate House*, "It's too late to change the past, but never too late to change the future." It's your future to change if you want. An eight-year-old young man whose wise mother (or his knowing older sister or aunt) read this book can make an early start to becoming a Man of Confi-Dance one day. A ninety-eight-year-old senior citizen living in a retirement home might read this book and realize how many ladies in this home would simply adore a Man of Confi-Dance living right there among them. And any man of any other age reading this book because his sixth sense told him that it might help him find what dancing can bring to his life must realize that he still has the rest of his life (his future) to make becoming a Man of Confi-Dance a reality. Whatever your age or your position in life, it is simply up to you now.

On the final page of Clive Cussler's thriller *White Death*, the hero, Kurt Austin, and a lovely young lady named Therri are having dinner aboard a huge zeppelin gliding in over Washington DC, and the final words of the novel are as follows:

"The pilot says we have time for one dance."

They rose from the table and Austin offered his arm, and they strolled into the dimly lit lounge. Austin turned on a record player and the mellow tunes of the Glenn Miller band flowed from the speaker. "Thought we should have a little period music."

Therri was staring out the observation window at the lights of the great East Coast megalopolis. She turned and said, "Thank you for an exceptional evening."

"It's not over yet. After we land, we can have a nightcap at my place. Who knows where the evening will lead."

"Oh, I know exactly where it will lead," she said with a dreamy smile.

He took her in his arms, inhaling the scent of her perfume, and high above the earth, they danced among the stars.

I wonder if Clive Cussler knew that Kurt Austin was such a Man of Confi-Dance.

APPENDIX A

A Waltz, By Any Other Name, Is Still A Pleasure

"When the music changes, so does the dance."
—African Proverb

LET'S VISIT THE different dances that a ballroom dancer begins with when first taking lessons and work our way up to the other dances that more experienced ballroom dancers enjoy. Remember, this book is not intended to teach you to dance, so this will be just a brief description of each dance to give you a little familiarity when you hear them or see them at lessons or at a dance venue. And instructors will vary in how they teach a particular dance. Most dances fit in one or the other of two main categories: smooth or Latin/rhythm. We'll begin with the basic smooth dances: *waltz, foxtrot, and tango.*

The waltz follows the line of dance (LOD) in that it is not danced in the same spot but requires the couple to move around the outside of the dance floor in a counterclockwise manner and is a wonderful smooth dance. At any level of competency, its cadence will always be slow-quick-quick (S-Q-Q). Beginners will often use a box step and not get too involved in the LOD until they get the feel of matching their steps with the musical measures. Many of the patterns that dancers use in the waltz can also be seen in the foxtrot, but they are still matched with the appropriate cadence of the music. Some of my favorite waltzes include "My Cup Runneth Over" by Ed Ames, or Anne Murray's "Could I Have This Dance?"

The foxtrot has always been the dance that I name when someone will ask me which of all the dances I like most. I really like them all, but the foxtrot is the one dance that comes to mind when I think of the elegance and grace that is exhibited when done well. The foxtrot also follows the LOD. The framing of the couple in closed position gives it the look that we think of when we picture true ballroom dancing as it was and indeed still is (think Fred Astaire and Ginger Rogers). At the basic level (Bronze), it repeats in a cadence of slow-slow-quick-quick (S-S-Q-Q) steps, and at the next level (Silver) the cadence changes to S-Q-Q. The two quick steps take up the same time frame as one slow step. Some of my favorite songs to dance the foxtrot are "A Nightingale Sang in Berkeley Square" by Bobby Darin and "You Make Me Feel So Young" by Frank Sinatra. Van Morrison's "Moon Dance" is another fine foxtrot.

The tango requires perhaps a little more work to master and employs the LOD with a cadence of S-S-Q-Q-Q. Many newcomers are taught to think of this cadence as One-Two Tang-O-Close with the Tango-O-Close taking up the same timing as the One-Two. The framing and positioning of hands is a little different in this dance as compared to the foxtrot or waltz and requires a little more patience by both partners to form a successful partnership. "Hernando's Hideaway" by the Johnson Brothers is a good tango as is "Por Una Cabeza" by Astor Piazolla and the Tango Project (from the movie *Scent of a Woman*).

Now we will review the basic dances for Latin/Rhythm: *rumba, cha cha, and swing.* All three of these dances are considered spot dances as they do not follow the LOD around the room and remain in the same general area of the dance floor throughout the dance. The music for most rumbas and cha chas is Latin, and the main movement that dancers aspire to master in these two is called Cuban motion, where the swaying of your hips is really the result of the placement of your feet and the shifting of your weight. But mastering Cuban motion is not done easily or overnight. It can take much work and years to get it where it comes to you naturally when the music begins.

The rumba can be a sexy dance, especially when the dancers keep good eye contact with each other. The basic rumba can begin with a box step, somewhat similar to the beginning box step taught in waltz, but the emphasis on the musical beat is different. Although still a S-Q-Q, some instructors prefer beginning on the first Q, thus Q-Q-S. It's the same music with the same box, only some like to begin on a S and others like to begin with a Q-Q. Remember, as in the foxtrot and waltz, the Q-Q takes up the same time as one S. Underarm turns, pivots, open breaks, and crossovers are all taught in the basic patterns once dancers have learned the basic box step and progress from there. Some good rumbas are Elvis Presley's "It's Now or Never" and much of the music by Antonio Carlos Jobim such as "Desafinado" or "Summer Wave."

The cha cha is a fun, energetic dance with a strong Latin beat and incorporates a cadence of "one-two-three-four-and, one-two-three-four-and, etc.," when the man begins with stepping to his left with his left foot. Nancy calls it the sassy dance. Beginners are often taught: one, two, cha, cha, cha. The same underarm turns, pivots, open breaks, and crossovers from the rumba are used in similar ways in the cha cha, and as in the rumba, you will progress from there. Marc Anthony's "I Need to Know" is a fine cha cha as is "Marino Sin Capitan" by Don Francisco or that lively song from the '60s, "Denise" by Randy and the Rainbows.

The swing (often referred to as East Coast swing or triple-step) is pretty much the basic jitterbug or fast dance that many of us learned in high school or college or somewhere else along the way. The trouble is, as I found, that we all grow up doing a fast dance like our peers, and this can vary from region to region and city to city all around this great big country of ours. The basic swing that ballroom dancers learn has the cadence of "one-two-three, one-two-three, rock step, one-two-three, one-two-three, rock step, etc." When the swing is referred to as the triple step, the cadence is learned as triple step, triple step, rock step, triple step, triple step, rock step, etc. When a really fast song is played such as "At the Hop" by Danny and the Juniors, dancers drop back to a single step version, which is simply "one, two, rock step, one, two, rock step, etc." This is because the music is too fast to get in a triple step in the time allotted in the measure of the beat. Good lively single step swing songs are "Rock Around the Clock" by Bill Haley and the Comets, and songs by Chuck Berry like "Johnny B. Goode" and "Sweet Little Sixteen," while a good triple step song would be Buddy Holley's "That'll Be the Day" or Bob Seeger's "Old Time Rock & Roll."

If you are learning these basic ballroom dances and practicing them anywhere, you are probably coming in contact with more advanced dancers that are doing other dances you like watching, and you will probably want to learn these too. And you can. And you will. The following are probably most of the ones to which I am referring.

Quickstep: an elegant dance much like a fast foxtrot with some steps unique to this dance, especially used in the corners of a rectangular dance floor to make the LOD work for you. When the more advanced dancers show off their quickstep (with plenty of open dance floor at their disposal), you will be wowed with their hopping and their skipping and their running and their incredibly fast footwork. This is a smooth dance normally competed at the international level.

Bolero:	a Latin spot dance much like the rumba but slightly slower, where the patterns are even more sexy and slinky and a pleasure to either observe or be dancing with a partner and performed in close body contact position.
Samba:	another Latin dance with a more robust tempo and usually a spot dance, but some dancers will do quite a bit of moving around the floor with the samba. The patterns can really move you down the dance floor with a cadence that is basically a "one-and-two, one-and-two," but the emphasis is much different than the cha cha, rumba, or bolero and can take a little more time to master. It's a dance that is technically difficult, combining rise and fall, sway, and Cuban motion, all at the same time and at speed.
Viennese Waltz:	a waltz but with a much faster tempo requiring different footwork in some places to maintain LOD while pivoting in what is called a "he go, she go" pattern. Of all of the ballroom dances, I consider this the toughest partner dance because of the heightened tempo of the music. Both partners can hear the music, feel the beat, but perhaps try to do their part just a little bit off of the tempo of the other, making it difficult to maintain the LOD. Wait awhile to begin learning this elegant dance.
West Coast Swing:	this dance came from the West Coast and spread east like many things do. It is like a spot dance in that you do not follow the LOD around the room, but it varies because it is danced in a slot. Each couple will stake out a slot on the dance floor and move up and down in that slot. The music is a slightly slower East Coast swing song and also employs the triple step idea, but in a different order: "one, two, one-two-three, one-two-three, one, two, one-two-three, one-two-three, etc." Some instructors will phrase as 1-2, 3-and-4, 5-and-6. There is no rock step here, and the final one-two-three in each measure is called the "anchor step." I love the WC swing because of its funky style and the opportunity to play with the steps and invent your own along the way. I call my style of WC swing "instant choreographing" and just go have fun when they play one of these dances. The '50s hit "Rockin' Pneumonia and the Boogie Woogie Flu" by Huey "Piano" Smith is a great WC swing song.

Raoul Weinstein

Merengue:	another dance with a Latin flavor but even easier to handle in that the cadence is a simple "one-a-one-a-one-a-one, etc." Or as I enjoy telling the ladies I dance with who are not sure they can do a merengue, "If you can count to one, you've got it made: one (and), one (and), etc. I don't consider the merengue to be a spot dance or one that follows an LOD, but one where I go all over the dance floor in no particular planned pattern. It is another dance where I just make it a fun dance with the ladies, throwing in steps from many of the other dances already discussed above. A little Latin emphasis with steps from a smooth dance can look completely different but still be familiar enough to your partner that you can lead it easily. Gloria Estefan's "Tres Deseos" from the movie *Dance with Me* is probably my favorite merengue.
Night Club Two Step:	this niche dance has come on the scene only in recent years and fills the void for dancing to songs with a slower tempo that do not fit the standard ballroom dances. When a slow song would be played by a band or at a club or lounge, ballroom dancers would be faced with the problem of what to dance to this song? The song wasn't quite right for a waltz or foxtrot or a rumba or bolero. It usually ended up being what we call a belly rubber dance, like we used to do in high school and throughout our lives to just hold your partner close and sway a little with the music right in place. Well, that's fine if you are with someone you'd like to do that with. But if you are a dance host and a song like that is played, it will probably be uncomfortable for one or both partners to get into a very close position on the dance floor. Enter the NC2S. It has become one of my favorite dances, and Nancy and I do quite well with it. In fact, I have been invited to co-host or lead several NC2S workshops in my areas of Florida, South Carolina, and on a recent dance cruise. The musical cadence used here is again the S-Q-Q but with a different basic step. In actuality, just about everything you will learn and use in the NC2S employs either the basic step, or the traveling step which is similar to one single step from the grapevine. It's fun and not that difficult to learn once you have mastered a few of the other basic ballroom dances. Chris DeBurgh's "Lady in Red" is one of the most popular songs for the NC2S. The NC2S can be used for such doo wop favorites like "In the Still of the Night" by the Five Satins and also successfully with many reggae songs like "Red, Red, Wine" by UB40.

Mambo: the mambo is of course another Latin dance and moves quite quickly. Most patterns are similar to those used in the rumba or even cha cha, but quicker, and with a little staccato mixed in. Like most Latin dances, it too is a spot dance. The secret, one which I have been pitiful in picking up and using with any reliability, is that the mambo starts on the two beat. That means you have to do the following: Listen to the intense music to discern quickly which beat is the one beat so that you can hold yourself (and your partner) from beginning on the more distinctive one beat, and then begin on the two beat. Thus, the mambo is danced to the following cadence: "hold, two, three, four, hold, two, three, four, etc."

For me, figuring out the two beat has always been difficult, and even if I am successful at the beginning, I rarely stay on the two beat very long. Fortunately for me, and I imagine for many others, the *Salsa* came along. Some may have a more detailed explanation of the salsa, but for me, the salsa in simply the mambo danced on the one beat. *Yea!* Instead of fearing whether or not I would find that elusive two beat, *now* I just get ready and when that wonderful one beat appears, I begin. I use anything you would use in the mambo, except that we are dancing the cadence "one, two, three, hold, one, two, three, hold, etc." And when I learned the NC2S, I found that almost everything I can do in this dance can also be employed in the salsa even though the salsa tempo is much faster, thus enlarging my repertoire in the salsa quite nicely.

Argentine Tango: this dance is sweeping across our continent originating in Argentina of course. It is danced to music familiar to us as tango music, but true Argentine tango music is a little different. If you already know tango, it will help, but it still takes getting used to. Men are taught to begin with their left foot in every other dance we learn, and then the instructor in the Argentine tango class tells us to begin on our *right* foot and go *back*, instead of forward as we also do in most every other dance. It is a beautiful and very sensuous dance to watch, and I hope one day to be able to feel that way by being an active participant.

APPENDIX B

Dancing: Here's To Your Health

"I see dance being used as a communication between body and soul to express what is too deep to find for words."
—Ruth St. Denis

I HAVE MADE REFERENCE several times in this book to the health benefits derived from dancing. For centuries, dance manuals and other writings have lauded the health benefits of dancing, usually as physical exercise. So of course when one considers the health benefits of dancing, one would normally be thinking of the physical benefits derived.

Whether it seems that way or not, dancing is intense aerobic exercise. This fact alone explains why ballroom dancing has such a positive effect on one's health. When I thought about which I would rather do: a strenuous boring hour on the treadmill or a fun and fast-paced hour of Latin dancing, you know which way I chose. And for most, I believe the latter is clearly more enticing (assuming you know how to do Latin dances). However, not only is dancing great for cardio, it is truly a whole body workout. Don't be surprised to wake up after a night of dancing, with all your muscles aching, though you are probably still smiling at the good dancing you enjoyed the night before. Out of many physical activities, dancing is considered to be one of the top five burning more calories than all but running. An average adult can burn between two hundred and five hundred calories during an hour of dancing depending on the intensity of the workout. Competitive dance workouts increase stamina, and many dances, both Latin and standard, improve flexibility and posture. In fact, dancing is a great sport for children with mild scoliosis as it may help to correct it.

Although ballroom dancing may not be as strenuous an activity as training to run a marathon, don't overlook the benefits of regular movement and exercise. The U.S. Department of Agriculture considers ballroom dancing a "moderate" activity. It has some specific health benefits that should be obvious such as muscle toning, conditioning, flexibility, and burning calories. Ballroom dancing helps tone and strengthen the muscles in your calves, thighs, and buttocks and also helps strengthen the core muscles of the abdomen and back. Specific ballroom dance moves work these muscles differently than more familiar exercises, such as walking, jogging, or cycling, do. If you're performing a style that involves lifting or dipping your partner, you can also get a pretty good upper-body workout.

As for conditioning, any regular exercise performed continuously for thirty to forty minutes three or four times a week will help condition your cardiovascular system, strengthen your heart, and lower your cholesterol and blood pressure. It will also increase your lung capacity and your general stamina. And as a weight-bearing exercise, dancing helps maintain bone density and can prevent osteoporosis. And one more conditioning benefit: dancing can also help rehabilitate your knees after surgery as it has a lower impact than jogging or aerobics.

Flexibility is an important part of being healthy, and, you guessed it, dancing requires a great amount of flexibility. Many dance classes begin with a warm-up including several stretching exercises. Dancers must strive to achieve full range of motion for all the major muscle groups. The greater the range of motion, the more muscles can flex and extend. Most forms of dancing require dancers to perform moves that employ bending and stretching, so dancers naturally become more flexible by simply dancing.

Now let's introduce another important finding: exercise releases endorphins, or feel-good chemicals into your bloodstream. This means that even a little dancing can improve your mood. A long, stressful, and tense day at work or school can be balanced with just half an hour of dancing. Since social dancing is an activity that one performs with a partner, it can also lessen loneliness and depression in the elderly.

Still, dancing can do more than just cure depression or help you lose weight and keep you in prime physical shape. Ballroom dancing is good for your brain; dancing apparently makes us smarter and is considered an excellent tool for reducing the chance of dementia and Alzheimer's disease because it is both a physical and social activity that requires a certain degree of memorization. This was found through a twenty-one-year study of senior citizens, seventy-five and older, led by the Albert Einstein College of Medicine in New York City, and funded by the National Institute on Aging. It was then published in the *New England Journal of Medicine* in 2003. Their method for objectively measuring mental acuity in aging was to monitor rates of dementia, including Alzheimer's. The study wanted to see if any physical or cognitive recreational activities influenced mental acuity. They discovered that some activities had a significant beneficial effect while other activities had none.

They studied cognitive activities such as reading books, writing for pleasure, doing crossword puzzles, playing cards, and playing musical instruments. They also studied physical activities like playing tennis or golf, swimming, bicycling, dancing, walking for exercise, and doing housework. One of the surprises of the study was that *almost* none of the physical activities appeared to offer any protection against dementia. There can be cardiovascular benefits of course, but the focus of this study was the mind. There was one important exception: the only physical activity to offer protection against dementia was frequent dancing. Here are the percentages of how much help the following activities helped: reading—35 percent, bicycling and swimming—0 percent, doing crossword puzzles at least four days a week—47 percent, playing golf—0 percent, and dancing frequently—76 percent (the greatest reduction of any activity studied, cognitive or physical). Can you think of a more enjoyable way for seniors to spend their recreational time than dancing when you read results like these?

I dance for a lot of reasons. I try to stay in shape to be able to perform at my best on the dance floor. Learning that dancing, in return, is very beneficial to my health in many ways is just icing on the cake. So whether you work out to be able to dance or you dance as a workout to stay in good shape, I raise a toast to all dancers, "Here's to your health!"

INDEX

A

adventure, 107
Ali (Weinstein's niece-in-law), 61-63
Andrews, Stan, 154
Argentine tango, 76, 194
Austen, Jane, 22
Austin, Kurt (*White Death* character), 188
Avila, Mario, 20, 155

B

Bachelor, The (TV show), 136
Barb, 82, 105, 116, 181
Baryshnikov, Mikhail, 125
Baudelaire, Charles, 70
Baum, Vicki, 15
Beckett, Samuel, 109
Bernie, 44
Berry, Chuck, 132, 191
Bill, 77
Blindt, Cyndi, 143-44
bolero, 192
Brando, Marlon, 28
Brown, James, 64

C

Carlin, George, 24
Chris (*Mixed Nuts* character), 147
Cohen, Leonard
    "Dance Me to the End of Love," 186-87
Coleman, Bill, 151

Cooke, Dean, 169
Cooper, Robert, 152
Corbett, Lennie, 132
Cosby, Gerald, 159
Cuban motion, 190
Cunard Line, 118, 135
Cussler, Clive
    White Death, 188

D

Dague, Bill, 66
Dague, Mary, 32, 70, 171
    backstory of, 66-68
dance
    clothing, 182-84
    and competition, 177, 179-81
    fear of, 21
    female viewpoint on, 93-96
    group lessons and, 70-71
    health benefits of, 165-97
    importance of practice in, 79-81
    insiders and outsiders in, 74-76
    joys of, 14
    and life, 186-88
        male and female cooperation in, 100-105
    male viewpoint on, 97-99
    probable reasons to, 65
    and romance, 85-86
    special moments with, 57-60
dance host
    benefits of a, 147
    requirements of a. *See various requirements*

"Dance Me to the End of Love" (Cohen), 186

Dancers at Sea (company), 19, 111, 114

Dancing Over the 7 Seas (company), 132

Date Night (film), 58

Dean, 41-43, 75, 168-69

Dedes, Konstantin "Dino," 51-52, 173

della Santina, Piero, 151-52

DeMille, Nelson
 Gate House, The, 187

Donna, 72

Doyle, Karen, 174-76

Duncan, Isadora, 182

DWTS (Dancing with the Stars), 13, 67, 186

E

ease with travel (requirement), 132-33

East Coast swing. *See under* swing

Edeling, Ben, 126, 153

Elvis, 47

Engberg, Elly, 35-36, 127, 129

Estridge, Benjamin Royce, 50

F

family status (requirement), 120

Fey, Tina, 58

finances (requirement), 120

Forsberg, Jon, 140

foxtrot, 189

G

Gate House, The (DeMille), 187

George (Mary Wile's nephew), 149

Gillian, 44

Gino, 82

Gino. *See* Tucci, Eugene "Gene"

Goodrich, Terri Lynn, 166-67

Graham, Martha, 48

Grogan, Donna, 72-73

H

Hale, Ed, 152

Haller, Barbara, 74

happiness, 55

Heart of Florida (USA Dance chapter), 166-67

Hopi Indian Saying, 87

J

Jacob (Weinstein's nephew), 61-63

Joan, 41, 44, 90, 148, 172-74

Johnson, Jimmy, 96

K

Karen, 77

Karen (Weinstein's sister), 76-78, 173

Keith (Weinstein's son), 91

Kline, Jeff and Sandy, 103

L

Larson, Barbara (she is an ex-fiancee), 34

Lee, Mama, 113

leisure time (requirement), 119

Let's Dance Cruises (company), 35, 127, 135

Lewis, Jerry Lee, 132

Linda (Weinstein's first wife), 24, 31-32, 105, 144

Lombardi, Vince, 184

Lorio, Joe, 171

loyalty (requirement), 133-34

Lundsford, Zane, 49

M

MacLaine, Shirley, 130

mambo, 194

Man of Confi-Dance
   aura of a, 163-65
   definition of a, 22
   job options of a, 139-46
   rules of etiquette of a, 159-62

Marilyn, 111

Mary, 11, 32, 34-35, 66-68, 70-71, 81-82, 104-5, 113-14, 135, 148-49, 165, 171, 177-78

Mary Worth (comic strip), 165

McMillon, Nancy, 9, 45, 89
   and the Argentine tango, 76
   meeting Raoul, 125-28

merengue, 193

Mille, Agnes de, 166

Miller, Joan, 41, 44, 90, 148, 172-74

Miller, Katey (*Dirty Dancing* character), 57

Moliere, 35

Moreth, Dale, 153

Morley, Christopher, 32

N

Nancy, 41, 111, 161, 168, 175

NC2S (night club two step), 61, 193

O

Obney, Richard "Dick," 154

O'Brien, Gale, 164

Olsen, Wendy, 111-12, 114-15, 128

P

Pelton, Linda Stata, 48-51

personal hygiene (requirement), 117

personality (requirement), 116

physical shape (requirement), 117

Q

Queen Mary II (ship), 113-14, 135

Queen Victoria (ship), 19, 135, 174

quickstep, 191

Quon, Don, 143

R

Rawls, Fitz, 174

Rhymes with Orange (comic strip), 95

Rios, Kevin, 52-53

Rogers, Ginger, 93, 189

rule follower (requirement), 132

rumba, 190

RW, 36-45

S

salsa, 194

samba, 192

Saunders, Jerry, 29

Scheffer, Tom, 150

self-esteem, 17, 20

shag (dance), 75-76

Shakespeare, William, 177

Sipe, Greg, 150-51
Smallowitz, Howard, 92
Smith, Austin Benjamin, 49
social skills (requirement), 119
South Carolina-Upstate (USA Dance chapter), 166
St. Denis, Ruth, 195
Sufi Saying, 97
Susan (Weinstein's second wife), 24, 32-33, 68, 70-71, 104-5, 177-79
swing
  East Coast, 75, 191
  West Coast, 75

T

tango, 190
team player (requirement), 121
Therri, 188
Tina, 155
Tom, 42-43, 147-50, 152, 155
Tootsie, 176
Trish, 45
Tucci, Eugene "Gene," 34, 81-82

U

ulterior motives, prohibition of (requirement), 123
USABDA (United States Amateur Ballroom Dancing Association). See USA Dance
USA Dance, 33, 35, 139, 144, 166-68

V

Viennese waltz, 104, 192

W

Walt, 72
waltz, 189
Ward, Walt and Jan, 72
wardrobe (requirement), 118-19
Wasserman, Horst, 153
Weinstein, Raoul L.
  beginnings with dance, 26-29
  as a dance host, 35-46, 109-15
  in high school and college, 30-31
    at his first dance competition, 177-79
  at his nephew's wedding, 61-63
  with Linda, 24, 31-32, 105, 144
  with Nancy, 90, 125-28
    as president of the Lakeland Association of Realtors, 170-72
  on the Queen Victoria, 19-20
  as a school dance judge, 48-53
  with Susan, 32-33, 68-69, 104
  with Terri Lynn, 167
  at Vail Village, 87-89
  at Vero Beach, 144-45
  at Walter Reed Middle School, 21
Wendy, 11, 43, 103, 111-12, 114-15, 122, 128, 131
West Coast swing. See under swing
White Death (Cussler), 188
Wile, Mary, 148-50
Witte, Bill (Weinstein's brother-in-law), 76-78
Wuennenberg, Dieter, 135-38, 180